Maat and Ancient Egyptian Magic

Unlocking Maat Philosophy and Kemetic Spirituality, along with Gods, Goddesses, and Spells of Ancient Egypt

© Copyright 2023 - All rights reserved.

The content contained within this book may not be reproduced, duplicated, or transmitted without direct written permission from the author or the publisher.

Under no circumstances will any blame or legal responsibility be held against the publisher, or author, for any damages, reparation, or monetary loss due to the information contained within this book, either directly or indirectly.

Legal Notice:

This book is copyright protected. It is only for personal use. You cannot amend, distribute, sell, use, quote, or paraphrase any part, or the content within this book, without the consent of the author or publisher.

Disclaimer Notice:

Please note the information contained within this document is for educational and entertainment purposes only. All effort has been executed to present accurate, up-to-date, reliable, complete information. No warranties of any kind are declared or implied. Readers acknowledge that the author is not engaging in the rendering of legal, financial, medical, or professional advice. The content within this book has been derived from various sources. Please consult a licensed professional before attempting any techniques outlined in this book.

By reading this document, the reader agrees that under no circumstances is the author responsible for any losses, direct or indirect, that are incurred as a result of the use of the information contained within this document, including, but not limited to, errors, omissions, or inaccuracies.

Your Free Gift
(only available for a limited time)

Thanks for getting this book! If you want to learn more about various spirituality topics, then join Mari Silva's community and get a free guided meditation MP3 for awakening your third eye. This guided meditation mp3 is designed to open and strengthen ones third eye so you can experience a higher state of consciousness. Simply visit the link below the image to get started.

https://spiritualityspot.com/meditation

Table of Contents

PART 1: MAAT 1
   INTRODUCTION 2
   CHAPTER 1: MAAT, GODDESS, AND SPIRITUALITY 4
   CHAPTER 2: MAAT AND KEMETICISM 14
   CHAPTER 3: THE 7 PRINCIPLES AND THE 42 LAWS 24
   CHAPTER 4: SACRED DEITIES AND HOW TO HONOR THEM 34
   CHAPTER 5: HONORING AKHU, OUR ANCESTORS 48
   CHAPTER 6: BUILDING A SHRINE 57
   CHAPTER 7: MAAT AND MAGICK 66
   CHAPTER 8: MAGICKAL CEREMONIES AND RITUALS 75
   CHAPTER 9: PRAYERS AND MEDITATIONS 84
   CHAPTER 10: ADDING MAAT INTO MODERN LIFE 89
   CONCLUSION 99
PART 2: ANCIENT EGYPTIAN MAGIC 101
   INTRODUCTION 102
   CHAPTER 1: ANCIENT EGYPTIANS AND MAGIC 104
   CHAPTER 2: CREATION, COSMOLOGY, AND PHILOSOPHY 110
   CHAPTER 3: MAJOR FEMALE DEITIES 118
   CHAPTER 4: MAJOR MALE DEITIES 136
   CHAPTER 5: EGYPTIAN SYMBOLS AND THEIR SIGNIFICANCE 152
   CHAPTER 6: EGYPTIAN AMULETS AND HOW TO MAKE THEM 162
   CHAPTER 7: MORE MAGICAL TOOLS TO CREATE 171
   CHAPTER 8: METHODS OF DIVINATION 180

CHAPTER 9: SACRED PLANTS AND HERBS 188
CHAPTER 10: ANCIENT EGYPTIAN SPELLS AND RITUALS 197
ANCIENT EGYPTIAN DEITIES A-Z 203
CONCLUSION 217
HERE'S ANOTHER BOOK BY MARI SILVA THAT YOU MIGHT LIKE 219
YOUR FREE GIFT (ONLY AVAILABLE FOR A LIMITED TIME) 220
REFERENCES 221

Part 1: Maat

The Ultimate Guide to Maat Philosophy, Principles, and Magick along with Kemetic Spirituality

Introduction

Maat is an ancient Egyptian goddess who represents truth, justice, balance, and order. She is often depicted as a woman with wings or as a Feather of Maat. As the goddess of truth, she helps us find truth and see things as they are. As the goddess of justice, she brings balance and order to our lives. And as the goddess of balance, she helps us maintain a healthy balance in all areas of our lives.

Maat is also a spiritual philosophy that teaches us that we are all connected and that we should live in harmony with each other and nature. The 7 Principles of Maat are guidelines for living a good life, and the 42 Laws of Maat are laws that everyone should follow to maintain balance and harmony in the world. These laws include things like honesty, respect for others, and taking care of the environment. The goal of the Maat philosophy is to help us live our lives in a way that is aligned with the natural order of the Universe.

Maat is an important part of Kemeticism, the ancient Egyptian religion. Kemeticism teaches that we are all children of the gods and must live our lives in a way that pleases them. To honor Maat, we can do many things. We can build shrines or altars for her in our homes, offer her prayers and meditations, and perform ceremonies and rituals in her name. We can also add her into our modern lives by living according to the principles of Maat and following its laws. By doing these things, we can create a more just and balanced world for everyone.

In this book, we will explore the goddess Maat, the spiritual philosophy of Maat, and how we can apply its principles in our own lives. We will also learn about some of the other Kemetic gods and goddesses and how we can honor them. We will also learn about building shrines, performing rituals and ceremonies, and using prayers and meditations to connect with the divine. And finally, we will explore how we can incorporate Maat into our modern lives.

This easy-to-follow guide will introduce you to the goddess Maat and its spiritual philosophy and provide the tools and techniques you need to incorporate it into your life. Whether you are new to Kemeticism or have been practicing for years, this book will help you deepen your understanding of this ancient tradition and apply its teachings. So, let us begin our journey into the world of Maat.

Chapter 1: Maat, Goddess, and Spirituality

From ancient Egypt comes the spiritual idea of Maat, represented by a goddess who stands for truth, order, morality, balance, justice, and more. Maat was a guiding principle in Egyptian society, and her name was invoked in various aspects of daily life. The hieroglyph for her name was often worn as an amulet, and people would take an oath in her name when seeking to tell the truth.

In the underworld, Maat was responsible for weighing the hearts of the dead to determine their worthiness when it came to entering the afterlife. Those who had led lives of imbalance and disorder were said to have their hearts "weighed down" with evil deeds, while those who had lived well, according to Maat, were said to have "light" hearts.

The concept of Maat helped create a society that was based on cooperation and harmony instead of one of chaos and violence. In this chapter, we will explore Maat's cultural and historical background and its relevance in modern times. We will also take a look at the origins of the goddess Maat, her roles, and various pieces of lore connected to her. Finally, we will discuss the importance of learning about Maat and how it can be applied to daily life.

Maat - The Spiritual Idea

Religion is a complex and often misunderstood topic. As humans, we are constantly searching for answers to life's big questions. What is our purpose? Where do we come from? Where do we go when we die? For many people, religion provides a framework for addressing these queries. There are countless religious traditions in the world, each with its own unique beliefs and practices. One of these traditions is Ancient Egyptian Religion. Central to this belief system was the goddess Maat.

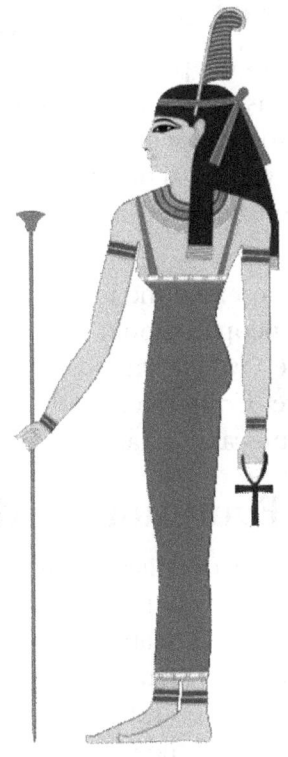

The goddess Maat represented truth and balance.
No machine-readable author provided. Jeff Dahl assumed (based on copyright claims)., CC BY-SA 4.0 <https://creativecommons.org/licenses/by-sa/4.0>, via Wikimedia Commons: https://commons.wikimedia.org/wiki/File:Maat.svg

Maat represented truth, justice, and balance. She was the force that held the universe together and ensured that everything remained in order. To the Egyptians, Maat was the spiritual ideal to which all individuals should aspire. In death, it was believed that one's heart would be weighed against a feather of Maat. If the heart was found to be lighter than the feather, then the person lived a virtuous life and would be granted access to the afterlife. If not, they would be cast into oblivion.

While the idea of Maat is no longer widely known, it remains an intriguing and thought-provoking concept. It offers a perspective on morality that is worth considering in our own lives. In a world where selfishness and greed often seem to triumph, the ideals of Maat provide a refreshing alternative. When we take the time to reflect on our actions and consider whether they align with Maat's principles, we may be surprised at how much more fulfilling our lives can be.

The Significance of Maat in Egyptian Culture

Ancient Egyptian culture was deeply rooted in spirituality, and one of the most important concepts was that of Maat. This principle of truth, justice, and balance was believed to be essential for maintaining harmony in both the natural and human worlds. The goddess Maat personified these qualities, and she was often depicted as a young woman with an ostrich feather on her head.

In many ways, Maat represented the ideal human being, and she served as a role model for how people should behave. The Egyptians thought that by living by Maat, they would stay in good favor with the gods and ensure a successful afterlife. Consequently, this concept was highly valued in Egyptian society and significantly shaped their culture.

The Evolution of Maat

The ancient Egyptian concept of Maat is often described as a system of moral principles or a code of conduct. The word Maat comes from the hieroglyphic symbol for an ostrich feather, which was used as a symbol of truth and justice in Egyptian iconography. The idea of Maat began with the belief that a set of divine laws upheld the Universe, and to maintain harmony between themselves and the natural world, humans had a duty to enforce these laws. Over time, the concept of Maat evolved to encompass ethical and moral principles. Eventually, it became synonymous with these concepts, and it continues to be an essential part of Egyptian culture today.

The Relevance of Maat in Modern Times

The ancient Egyptians had a complex and sophisticated religion that revolved around the worship of a pantheon of gods and goddesses. In many ways, Maat was the Egyptian equivalent of the Greek goddess Nike or the Roman goddess Justitia. For the ancient Egyptians, Maat was not simply a moral code or ethical system but was a cosmic force that ensured that the universe continued to function properly. In times of chaos or disorder, it was believed that Maat could be restored through ritual and prayer.

Despite being an ancient concept, Maat is still relevant in modern times. In a world that is often chaotic and unpredictable, we can all benefit from a reminder to seek truth, justice, and balance. We can also learn from the example of the ancient Egyptians, who saw Maat as a powerful force for good in the world. By invoking Maat in our own lives, we can help create a more just and orderly world for ourselves and future generations.

The Goddess Maat

In ancient Egyptian mythology, Maat was the goddess of truth, justice, and order. She was often depicted as a young woman wearing a white feather representing truth. Maat was the daughter of the sun god Ra and the sky goddess Nut. In some stories, she was also the wife of the moon god Thoth. Maat was believed to keep the world in balance and prevent chaos. Her name meant "truth" or "justice."

Egyptians believed that if they followed Maat's laws, they would be rewarded in the afterlife. Those who did not follow her laws would be punished. Maat's priests were responsible for ensuring that people followed her laws. They also helped to settle disputes and administer punishment. The goddess represented everything good and right in Egyptian culture.

The Origins of the Goddess Maat

The goddess Maat is thought to have originated in the Predynastic Period of Egyptian history. During this time, the people of Egypt were divided into two major groups, the nomadic herders of the desert and the sedentary farmers of the Nile Valley. The two groups had different beliefs and customs, and they often came into conflict with one another. The desert nomads worshipped a goddess known as the "Eye of Ra." This goddess was associated with chaos and disorder. The farmers of the Nile Valley worshipped a goddess known as "Maat." This goddess was associated with truth, justice, and balance.

As the two groups came into contact with one another, they began to share their beliefs and customs. The Eye of Ra became associated with Maat, and the two goddesses merged into one. Over time, the concept of Maat came to encompass all that was good and right in the universe. It was believed that humans were obliged to uphold Maat's laws to maintain harmony between themselves and the natural world.

The Roles of the Goddess Maat

The feather that Maat was often depicted wearing represented truth and was used as a symbol for this goddess in art and literature. Maat was also sometimes shown with an ostrich feather or a pair of scales. These symbols represented her role as the goddess of truth and justice.

In ancient Egyptian mythology, she played an important role in the afterlife. The dead were judged by Osiris, who placed their hearts on a scale and weighed them against a feather. If the heart was heavier than the feather, it meant that the person had committed evil deeds in life and that they would be destroyed.

As the goddess of truth and justice, it is no surprise that Maat was also worshipped as the patroness of scribes and judges. In ancient Egypt, these roles were closely intertwined, as scribes were responsible for recording legal decisions and maintaining accurate records. The goddess Maat represented order and balance in the universe, and her cult was particularly popular among those who relied on these principles in their work. Scribes and judges invoked her name when taking oaths, and her image was often placed in courtrooms as a reminder of the importance of truth and fairness. By honoring Maat, scribes and judges ensured that they would be blessed with wisdom and insight in their work.

Offerings were made to her to preserve truth and justice in society. She is even said to have created the universe itself in some myths. As such, she was a powerful and important goddess in ancient Egyptian religion.

Lore Connected to the Goddess Maat

There are many tales and stories connected to the goddess Maat. From her role in the creation of the universe to her place in the afterlife, she was an important part of Egyptian mythology. Here are some of the most popular tales associated with this goddess:

Creation of the Universe

One story claims that Maat was responsible for the creation of the universe. In this tale, she is said to have emerged from the primeval waters with the sun god Ra. Together, they created the first land and all the creatures that inhabit it. This story highlights Maat's role as the goddess of truth and balance. It also emphasizes her importance in the creation of the world.

The Tale of the Two Fighters

In this story, two men get into a fight. One of the men was killed, and the other was brought before a judge; when the judge asked the man what had happened, he said he did not remember. The judge then summoned the goddess Maat. Maat told the judge what had happened: the first man started the fight, and the second man only defended himself. The judge then pronounced the second man innocent and set him free.

This story illustrates the importance of truth in Egyptian society. It also shows that even if someone is unsure what happened, the goddess Maat will always reveal the truth.

The Destruction of Apep

Apep was a giant serpent who lived in the underworld. Every night, he would try to destroy the sun god Ra. To protect Ra, the goddess Maat fought Apep. She used her sword to cut off his head then she destroyed his body with her ferocious lion. This story highlights Maat's role as the protector of Ra. It also shows her strength and power.

The Judgment of Set

According to legend, Maat was responsible for maintaining the cosmic order and ensuring that the universe remained in balance. One of her most famous stories is known as the "Judgment of Set." Set was the god of chaos and disorder. In this story, he killed his brother Osiris and took over Egypt. Ra was so angry that he sent Maat to judge Set.

This tale tells how Maat is called upon to judge the deeds of the god Set, who is accused of murdering his brother Osiris. After carefully considering the evidence, Maat pronounced Set guilty and condemned him to eternal punishment. The story of the Judgment of Set teaches us that even gods must answer for their actions and that justice will always prevail.

Maat in Contrast to Isfet

In contrast to Maat, Isfet was the goddess of chaos, violence, and disorder. She was often depicted as a lioness or a serpent, and her name meant " injustice." Isfet was believed to cause 13 diseases, 42 types of evil, and everything that was unpleasant in life. She was also thought to be responsible for natural disasters like floods and storms. While Maat represented all that was good and orderly in the world, Isfet represented everything chaotic and dangerous.

In Egyptian mythology, Maat and Isfet were constantly in conflict with each other. The Egyptians believed that if Maat lost this battle, the world would be plunged into chaos and darkness. But if Maat won, the world would remain in balance and harmony. The story of the Judgment of Set is an example of Maat's victory over Isfet. Set is punished for his chaotic and violent actions in this story, and Maat is reaffirmed as the goddess of truth and justice.

The Importance of Learning about Maat

For the ancient Egyptians, Maat was essential to both individual and societal well-being. Learning about her can teach us a lot about how to live our lives in a harmonious and fulfilling way. It can also help us understand our role in the world around us. By learning about Maat, we can gain a greater sense of purpose and meaning in our lives.

In our modern world, it can be easy to forget about the importance of truth, justice, and balance. We may get caught up in our own lives and neglect the needs of others. We may also allow our desires and fears to cloud our judgment. But if we take the time to reflect on the teachings of Maat, we can learn how to live our lives in a more harmonious and fulfilling way. Some of the things that we can do to apply the principles of Maat to our lives include:

Treating Others with Respect and Fairness

Treating others with respect and fairness can help create a more just and balanced world. Of course, this is not always easy. We all have different perspectives and opinions, and it can be difficult to find common ground. However, if we remember the principles of Maat, we can treat each other with kindness and understanding, even when we disagree. Doing so can help create a more peaceful and harmonious world.

We act according to Maat's principle when we treat others with respect and fairness. This means we are considering their needs and feelings and giving them the same treatment we would want for ourselves. It also means that we are not taking advantage of them or mistreating them in any way.

Being Honest and Truthful

While the concept of Maat is thousands of years old, its message is still relevant today. In our fast-paced, constantly connected world, it can be easy to get caught up in lies and half-truths. But if we take a moment to pause and reflect on the goddess Maat, we can be reminded of the importance of living an honest and truthful life. This means that we should not lie or cheat. We should also be careful not to make promises we cannot keep. When we are honest, we are being fair to both ourselves and others.

Respecting the Rights of Others

Another important aspect of Maat is respect for the rights of others. This means we should not take advantage of others or infringe on their rights. We should also be careful not to overstep boundaries. We all have the right to live our lives in peace and harmony. We all have a personal responsibility to uphold the principles of Maat in our daily lives. The principles of Maat provide a moral compass that can help us make choices that align with our highest values. By following the path of Maat, we can create a more just and peaceful world for ourselves and generations to come.

Living in Sync with This World

Many people feel disconnected from the world around them. They live in a state of imbalance, feeling that they are at odds with the natural order of things. This can lead to a sense of frustration and even despair. However, there is an ancient Egyptian philosophy that can help us find harmony with the world around us. The principle of Maat teaches us to act with integrity and to respect the rights of others. By following this philosophy, we can learn to live in sync with the world around us and find a sense of peace and fulfillment.

The Benefits of Learning about Maat

Learning about Maat can offer numerous benefits. For one, it can help foster a greater understanding and appreciation for justice and morality. Additionally, studying Maat can give insights into how the ancient Egyptians viewed the world and their place within it. As such, learning about Maat can be a valuable experience for anyone interested in history or comparative religion. Here are some additional benefits of learning about Maat:

1. Harmonious and Fulfilling Lives

The Maat Principles are a set of guidelines that offer advice on how to live a harmonious and fulfilling life. These principles can help us create balance in our lives and relationships based on the teachings of Ancient Egyptian wisdom. By learning about Maat, we can develop a greater understanding of ourselves and the world around us. The Maat Principles offer a valuable perspective on how to live our lives in a respectful, compassionate, and just way. They provide us with a blueprint for how to create more harmony and fulfillment in our lives.

2. A Deeper Understanding of Egyptian History and Culture

Maat represents the ideal order of the universe, and her name is also used to refer to the concept of truth and justice. The importance of Maat was emphasized in Egyptian society, and it was believed that she should be included in every aspect of life. By learning about Maat, we can gain a deeper understanding of Egyptian history and culture. We can learn about the importance of justice and truth in Ancient Egyptian society. Additionally, we can explore the role that Maat played in shaping Egyptian religion and philosophy.

3. A Greater Appreciation for Justice and Morality

When we learn about the goddess Maat, we gain a greater appreciation for justice and morality. The Egyptians believed that it was important to live in harmony with Maat and that this would bring about a just and orderly world. Consequently, they placed a great emphasis on law and morality. By understanding Maat, we can better appreciate the importance of justice and morality in our own lives. We can also gain a greater understanding of the Ancient Egyptian worldview and how they strove to create a just society. Consequently, learning about Maat can help us to be better people in the present day.

4. The Path to a More Peaceful and Just World

The principles of Maat were based on the belief that all people are equal and should be treated fairly. By understanding and upholding these ideals, we can create a more compassionate society. In addition, learning about Maat can also help us find inner peace. When we live by her principles, we can find balance and harmony within ourselves. As a result, we are better able to deal with the stresses of daily life. Ultimately, that can lead us down the path to a more peaceful and just world.

5. A Greater Understanding of the Self

The Ancient Egyptians believed that each person had a Ka or spiritual double. The Ka was thought to be the essence of a person's personality and to represent their deepest desires. Consequently, it was believed that by understanding one's Ka, one could gain a greater understanding of themselves. Learning about Maat can help us better understand our own Ka.

Maat is an important goddess in Egyptian mythology and religion. She represents the ideal order of the universe and is associated with truth, justice, and balance. Learning about Maat can be a valuable experience for anyone interested in history or comparative religion. Additionally, it can also help us live more harmonious and fulfilling lives. Finally, understanding Maat can lead us down the path to a more peaceful and just world.

Chapter 2: Maat and Kemeticism

Maat plays a central role in Kemetism, as it does in ancient Egyptian religion. Maat represents the ideal of harmony and order in the universe as the goddess of truth, justice, and balance. In Kemetism, she is central to our understanding of the world and our place within it. By living by her principles, we can create a more peaceful and equitable world for all.

This chapter will explore the beliefs and traditions of Kemetism, with a focus on the importance of Maat. We will also compare Kemetism to Christianity, highlighting the similarities and differences between the two religions.

What Is Kemetism?

Kemetism, also known as Egyptian Neopaganism or Kemetic Orthodoxy, is a modern Pagan religious movement based on ancient Egyptian religion. Kemetism traces its roots back to the early 1900s when Egyptology first emerged as a field of study. Interest in ancient Egyptian religion grew throughout the 20th century, eventually leading to the formation of various Kemetic organizations and groups in the 1970s and 80s.

The Origins of Kemetism

In the 19th century, several scholars began rediscovering and reviving ancient Egyptian religion. These "Egyptologists" included the British archaeologist Sir Flinders Petrie, the French Egyptologist Auguste Mariette, and the German Egyptologist Karl Richard Lepsius. They were able to decipher hieroglyphics and learn about ancient Egyptian beliefs and practices. This led to a greater understanding and appreciation of ancient Egyptian religion.

The Development of Kemetism

During the early 20th century, several occult groups began to adopt aspects of ancient Egyptian religion into their belief systems. This includes the Hermetic Order of the Golden Dawn, which was influential in the development of modern Wicca, and the Ordo Templi Orientis, which is still active today.

However, it was not until the 1970s and 80s that Kemeticism began to emerge as a distinct religious movement. This was largely due to the work of two American Egyptologists, Ronald L. Grimes and Tamara L. Siuda. Grimes is the author of several books on Kemeticism, including The Discovery of the Goddess and The Pagan Faith of Rameses the Great. Siuda is the founder of the Kemetic Orthodoxy, the largest and most well-known Kemetic organization.

Kemetism Today

Today, Kemetism is practiced by a small but growing number of people worldwide. Kemetists often worship together in temples or as part of an online community. While no one unified Kemetic theology exists, most Kemetists believe in the power of the gods and goddesses to influence the world and our lives. Many Kemetists also participate in regular rituals and ceremonies, sometimes involving animal sacrifice. Kemetism is not just a religion but a way of life for many who follow it. It provides a connection to the past and a sense of belonging to a larger community.

The Beliefs and Traditions of Kemetism

Kemetism is a modern pagan religion that centers on the worship of ancient Egyptian gods and goddesses. Its followers believe that by reconnecting with the religion of their ancestors, they can create a more balanced and harmonious world. The Kemetic name for Egypt is Kemet, which means "the black land." This refers to the fertile soil along the Nile River, which was the center of Egyptian civilization.

The Kemetic year begins in September and ends in August. This calendar is based on the agricultural cycle of the Nile River, which floods annually between June and September. The Kemetic day begins at sunrise and ends at sunset. There are three main pillars of Kemetism, Maat,

Netjer, and Ancestors.

Maat is the principle of truth, justice, and balance and is represented by the feather of Maat, which was used to weigh the hearts of deceased Egyptians in the afterlife. Netjer is the Kemetic word for god or goddess. Ancestors are those who have gone before us and who continue to play an important role in our lives. Kemetism teaches that we are all interconnected and must always strive to live in harmony with each other and nature.

The Gods and Goddesses

One thing that makes Kemetism unique is its pantheon of gods and goddesses. Some of the most popular deities include Isis, Osiris, and Ra.

Isis

Isis was one of the most popular gods and goddesses of ancient Kemetism. She was worshipped across Egypt, and her temples were some of the most visited in the country. Isis was associated with several different concepts, including motherhood, fertility, magic, and healing. Her symbols included the ankh, lotus flower, the cow, and the papyrus plant. Isis was often shown as a woman with wings or as a woman with cow's horns on her head.

Osiris

In Kemetism, Osiris is the god of the underworld and the afterlife. He is often depicted as a green-skinned man with a pharaoh's beard, wearing a crown of feathers and holding a staff. Osiris is the husband of Isis and the father of Horus. Osiris was murdered by his brother Set but was resurrected by Isis and became the judge of the dead in the afterlife.

Osiris is the lord of fertility and agriculture, and as such, he is often associated with the Nile River. He is also associated with death and resurrection, as he was resurrected after being killed by Set. Many Kemetists believe that when they die, they will be judged by Osiris in the afterlife and, depending on their deeds in life, granted a place in either the Field of Reeds or the Devourer's Mouth. As such, Osiris is an important god to many Kemetists, who view him as a powerful protector and guide.

Ra

Ra is the ancient Egyptian god of the sun and one of the most important gods in the Kemetic pantheon. Ra was believed to be the creator of the universe, and his image was often carved into temple walls and obelisks. He was also associated with royalty, and his name was often used as a royal title. Ra was usually depicted as a man with the head of a sun disk or as a hawk-headed lion. He was sometimes also shown with a human body and was always accompanied by his faithful companions, the goddesses Maat and Isis.

Ra was believed to travel across the sky in his solar bark and descend into the underworld at night. The Egyptians believed that Ra continued to watch over them even after death and that he would judge their souls in the afterlife. As such, he was one of the most powerful and important gods in Kemetism.

Horus

In the ancient Egyptian religion, Horus was the god of the sky and the king of the gods. He was often depicted as a falcon-headed man wearing the crown of Upper Egypt. As the son of Osiris and Isis, Horus was also associated with the sun and with healing. In one of his most famous myths, Horus battled against his uncle, Set, for control of Egypt. This myth symbolized the struggle between order and chaos, and it helped to explain why the Pharaoh was believed to be divine.

Today, Horus is still venerated by followers of Kemetism, an Egyptian-inspired religion that emerged in the early twentieth century. Devotees believe that Horus can help them overcome challenges and achieve their highest potential.

Thoth

Kemetism is an ancient Egyptian religion that centers on the worship of a pantheon of gods and goddesses. One of the most important deities in Kemetism is Thoth, who is often depicted as an ibis-headed man. Thoth is the god of wisdom, magic, and writing and is said to have invented hieroglyphs.

Thoth is also associated with the moon and is sometimes referred to as the "Lord of the Moon." In addition to these associations, Thoth is also one of the most important gods in the Kemetian afterlife, where he acts as a guide and protector for the dead. As such, he is a greatly revered deity in Kemetism, and his temples are some of Egypt's most popular tourist destinations.

Bast

In Kemetism, Bast is a goddess of the sun, cats, warmth, and fertility. She is often depicted as a woman with the head of a cat or lioness, and she is sometimes known as the "Eye of Ra." In addition to her role as a solar deity, Bast is also associated with cats and other felines. She is often said to lead them in their nightly hunts, and she is also thought to be the protectress of cats and their keepers.

Bast is also a goddess of love and fertility, and her temples were often used as places of healing. Those who worshipped her believed that she had the power to cure diseases and bring new life into the world. As a result, Bast was one of the most popular goddesses in ancient Kemet.

Afterlife in Kemetism

According to Kemetic teachings, the soul is immortal and will live on in the afterlife. There is no single idea of what the afterlife looks like, but it is often thought of as a paradise where the soul can rest and be at peace. The journey to the afterlife is not always easy, but the soul must pass through several tests before reaching its final destination.

Some of these tests are said to be difficult, but passing through them is seen as a sign of strength and perseverance. Those who successfully navigate the afterlife are thought to be rewarded with eternal life in paradise. For many Kemetics, the belief in life after death is one of the most comforting aspects of their religion. It gives them hope that even after they die, their souls will continue to exist in some form and that they will someday be reunited with their loved ones.

Rituals and Ceremonies

Kemetism is an ancient Egyptian religion that has been practiced for over 5,000 years. Throughout this time, it has developed a rich tradition of rituals and ceremonies that are still practiced by its modern-day followers. Here are some of the most important rituals and ceremonies in Kemetism:

The Opening of the Mouth Ceremony

The Opening of the Mouth ceremony is one of the most important rituals in Kemetism, a religion based on the worship of ancient Egyptian gods and goddesses. The ceremony is used to consecrate images of the gods and bring them to life so that they can be worshipped. The ritual involves two priests, one representing the god Shu and the other representing the goddess Tefnut.

Shu holds a ceremonial adze which he uses to open the mouth of the statue or image. Tefnut then breathes life into the image using an incense burner. The Opening of the Mouth ceremony is often performed on statues of Osiris as it is believed that this will allow him to resurrect and fulfill his role as lord of the underworld. The ceremony can also be performed on mummies giving them the ability to speak and see in the afterlife.

Festival of Bast

The Festival of Bast is one of the most important holidays in Kemetism, a religion based on the worship of the Egyptian goddess Bast. Held every year on the first day of the month of Thoth, the festival celebrates Bast's role as a protector and guardian. During the festival, devotees of Bast offer prayers and sacrifices to her and often wear special clothing or jewelry in her honor. The holiday is also a time for feasting and merriment, and many Kemetic temples hold public celebrations that include music, dance, and feasts of traditional foods. For those who worship Bast, the Festival of Bast is a time to remember her as a powerful deity who brings strength and protection to her followers.

The Festival of Opet

The Festival of Opet was one of the most important Ancient Egyptian ceremonies. It lasted for over two weeks and was held in honor of the god Amun, his consort Mut and their son Khonsu. During the festival, a statue of Amun was carried down the river Nile on a barge from his temple at Karnak to Luxor. Along the way, there were feasts, music, and dancing. The statue was placed in a shrine at Luxor, where it stayed for a week. Then, it was brought back to Karnak in a grand procession. The festival was a time of joy and celebration, strengthening the bond between the people and their gods.

The Mesektet Boat Races

The Mesektet Boat Races are a popular ritual among followers of Kemetism, an ancient Egyptian religion. The races take place on the fifth day of the month of Epip, when the sun god Ra is believed to be at its weakest. During the race, participants try to reach the finish line in boats shaped like papyrus barges. The winner is said to be blessed by Ra and is given a special place in the temple of Re-Horakhty.

The Mesektet Boat Races are just one of many rituals and ceremonies that play an important role in Kemetism. Others include the Opening of the Mouth ceremony, which is used to bring statues and mummies to life, and the Festival of Opet, which celebrates the union of Osiris and Isis. Together, these rituals and ceremonies create a strong sense of community among followers of Kemetism and provide a way to connect with their ancient beliefs.

Ethics and Morality

Ethics and morality are two important concepts in any society. They define what is right and wrong and provide a common set of guidelines that people can use to make decisions. Kemetism is an African ethical and moral system that is based on the teachings of the ancient Egyptian priesthood. The Kemetic code of ethics stresses Maat, or balance and harmony. This means that individuals must strive to maintain balance in all areas of their lives, including their relationships with other people, nature, and the divine.

In addition, Kemetics believe that every action has a consequence, both good and bad. This belief helps guide people in their decision-making, as they consider the immediate consequences of their actions and the long-term implications. By following the principles of Maat, Kemetics strive to create a just and harmonious world for all.

The Philosophy of Kemetism

Kemetism is a relatively new faith based on the belief that the gods and goddesses of ancient Egypt were still very much alive and active in the world. Followers of Kemetism believe that it is possible to commune with these deities and that they can offer guidance and protection in our lives. Kemetism's philosophy is founded on Maat's principles, which emphasize balance, truth, justice, and order.

Kemetism's philosophy emphasizes justice.
Ahmer Jamil Khan, CC0, via Wikimedia Commons:
https://commons.wikimedia.org/wiki/File:Scales_of_Justice_and_Wreath.svg

The Kemetists think that by adhering to these standards, the world may become a more peaceful place. In addition, Kemetists seek to connect with their ancestors and the spirit world and tap into the wisdom of those who have gone before. By honoring our past and present, Kemetists believe that we can create a bright future for all.

The Role of the Priesthood in Kemetism

The ancient Egyptian priesthood played a very important role in society. They were responsible for keeping the temples clean and running smoothly and performing various ceremonies and rituals. The priesthood was also responsible for teaching people about the gods and goddesses and helping them understand Maat's principles.

In modern times, the Kemetic priesthood is not as large or as organized as it once was. However, there are still a few priests and priestesses who practice the faith and who strive to keep the traditions alive. These individuals play an important role in the Kemetist community, providing guidance and wisdom to those who seek them.

The Importance of Maat in Kemetism

One of the most important concepts in Kemetism is Maat, which roughly translates to order, balance, or justice. The idea of Maat is central to ancient Egyptian morality, and it dictates that individuals should live in harmony with one another and with the natural world. In practical terms, this means that people should act with honesty, compassion, and respect. Furthermore, they should strive to maintain balance in all aspects of their lives.

The principle of Maat is often represented by the image of a scale, with one side representing chaos and the other side representing order. The goal is to keep the scales in balance so that neither side tips too far. This can be a difficult task, but it is one that Kemetics believe is worth striving for.

While the concept of Maat might seem simple at first glance, it can be difficult to put into practice. However, those who try to live by Maat often find their lives more fulfilling and meaningful. Additionally, by living in harmony with others, they help create a more just and peaceful world. In short, the concept of Maat is essential for both individual well-being and the health of society as a whole.

Kemetism vs. Christianity

One of the main reasons for Kemetism's resurgence is the fact that it is not tied to any one culture or ethnicity. Rather, Kemetism is open to anyone who seeks to connect with the divine through the teachings of Maat. In contrast, Christianity is a religion largely based on the belief in one God.

While there are many different branches of Christianity, the central tenets remain the same - faith in Jesus Christ as the savior and adhering to His word. For many people, Kemetism offers a more tolerant and inclusive path to spirituality than Christianity. In a world that is increasingly divided, Kemetism provides a unique opportunity for people of all backgrounds to come together and worship as one.

Similarities

Although often overshadowed by Christianity, Kemetism shares several similarities. Here are just a few:

- Both Kemetism and Christianity believe in the existence of one or more gods.
- Both religions teach that living a good and moral life is important.
- Both Kemetism and Christianity emphasize the importance of community.
- Both faiths teach that it is possible to commune with the divine.
- Both Kemetism and Christianity view suffering as a necessary part of the human experience.

Differences

Despite some shared beliefs, however, Kemetism and Christianity remain quite different from one another. While Kemetism focuses on inner transformation, Christianity is primarily concerned with salvation from sin.

Kemetism and Christianity are two distinct religions. Kemetism is based on the belief that there is one Supreme God who is responsible for everything in the universe. Christianity, on the other hand, teaches that there is a Trinity of three separate but equal gods. Christians also believe in the concept of original sin, while Kemetics do not.

Finally, Kemetics follow strict dietary laws and practice ritual cleansing, while Christians do not. While there are many differences between these two religions, they both offer a path to spirituality and a way to connect with the divine.

Kemetism is an ancient religion that focuses on the goddess Maat and the concept of balance. This religion has seen a resurgence in recent years due to its inclusive and tolerant nature. The rituals and beliefs of Kemetism include a focus on nature, the afterlife, and morality. Kemetism is a complex religion that is still being studied and practiced by many people today.

This chapter has provided an overview of Maat and Kemeticism. We have explored this unique religion's history, beliefs, and practices. In conclusion, Kemetism is a valuable spiritual tradition that has much to offer the modern world.

Chapter 3: The 7 Principles and the 42 Laws

The ancient Egyptians believed in several things that many would see as mere superstitions. They believed in gods and goddesses that ruled over different aspects of their lives and in an afterlife where they would be judged on their deeds in this life. The ancient Egyptians had a code of conduct that they believed would help them lead their lives in such a way that they would be judged favorably in the afterlife. This code of conduct was known as Maat.

This chapter will provide an overview of Maat and the 7 principles that she represented. In addition, this chapter will explore the connection between Maat and the 10 commandments, as well as the 42 laws that were associated with her. Finally, the chapter will discuss how following the laws of Maat was thought to help one achieve a peaceful afterlife.

The 7 Principles of Maat

The ancient Egyptians had a complex belief system that revolved around the idea of balance. This principle was known as Maat, and was reflected in all aspects of Egyptian life. The 7 Principles of Maat were a set of guidelines that outlined how individuals could live in harmony with themselves and their community. These principles encouraged truthfulness, justice, and compassion and helped create a society based on respect and cooperation. The 7 Principles of Maat remain an inspiring example of how different cultures can promote peace and balance in the world. Here is a brief overview of each principle:

1. Truth

The first principle of Maat is truth. In Ancient Egyptian beliefs, the first principle of Maat emphasizes the importance of truthfulness in all aspects of life. Honesty is believed to be essential for creating and maintaining relationships and achieving success in any endeavor. By speaking and acting with integrity, we can align ourselves with the Universe and manifest our deepest desires. When we are truthful, we are in alignment with our highest selves and the Divine will.

The Feather of Maat represents the principal of truth.
Metropolitan Museum of Art, CC0, via Wikimedia Commons:
https://commons.wikimedia.org/wiki/File:Scarab_Inscribed_with_a_Maat_Feather_MET_11.215.2_2_bottom.jpg

This principle is represented by the Feather of Maat, which was used in the ancient Egyptian ceremony of The Weighing of the Heart. In this ceremony, the hearts of the dead were weighed against a feather to symbolize the importance of truth in the afterlife. Those who had lived their lives with integrity and had been truthful to themselves and others were thought to have light hearts that could easily balance against the feather. Those who had led lives full of deception and lies were thought to have heavy hearts that would weigh down the balance.

2. Justice

The second principle of Maat is justice. In Ancient Egyptian beliefs, the second principle of Maat emphasizes the importance of fairness in all aspects of life. It is believed that everyone should be treated equitably and that no one should receive preferential treatment. This principle encourages us to stand up for what is right, even when it is difficult, and to always fight for a fair and just world.

This principle is represented by the Scalpel of Maat, which was used in the ancient Egyptian ceremony of The Opening of the Mouth. In this ceremony, the mouth of the deceased was opened so they could speak in the afterlife. The scalpel symbolized the need for justice to create a balance in the Universe. Those who had fought for justice in their lives were thought to have their mouths open in the afterlife. Those who had oppressed others were thought to have their mouths sealed shut.

3. Balance

The third principle of Maat is balance. In Ancient Egyptian beliefs, this principle emphasizes the importance of maintaining equilibrium in all aspects of life. It is believed that everything exists in a state of balance and that this equilibrium should be respected. This principle encourages us to create harmony in our lives and to avoid excessive behaviors that can lead to imbalance.

This principle is represented by the Scales of Maat, used in the ancient Egyptian ceremony of The Weighing of the Heart. In this ceremony, the hearts of the dead were weighed against a feather to symbolize the need for balance in the afterlife. Those who had lived their lives in harmony with themselves and their community were thought to have light hearts that would easily be able to balance against the feather. Those who had led lives of chaos and disorder were thought to have heavy hearts that would weigh down the balance against the feather.

4. Order

The fourth principle of Maat is order. In Ancient Egyptian beliefs, the fourth principle of Maat emphasizes the importance of organization in all aspects of life. It is believed that a well-ordered life leads to a well-ordered universe. This principle encourages us to keep our lives in order to create the most harmonious world possible.

This principle is represented by the Scepter of Maat, which was used in the ancient Egyptian ceremony of The Weighing of the Heart. In this ceremony, the hearts of the dead were weighed against a feather to symbolize the need for balance in the afterlife. Those who had led well-ordered lives were thought to have light hearts that would easily be able to balance against the feather. Those who had led lives of chaos and disorder were thought to have heavy hearts that would weigh down the balance against the feather.

5. Harmony

The fifth principle of Maat is harmony. In Ancient Egyptian beliefs, the fifth principle of Maat emphasizes the importance of living in harmony with oneself, others, and the environment. It is believed that harmonious relationships lead to a well-ordered universe. This principle, represented by the Ostrich Feather of Maat, encourages us to build relationships based on respect and understanding so that we can create the most balanced world possible.

On a personal level, this principle refers to the need to balance our lives and avoid becoming too attached to material possessions. This includes maintaining a healthy lifestyle, spending time with loved ones, and giving back to the community. On a larger scale, harmony refers to the need to maintain balance in the world around us. This includes respecting the natural environment, working towards social justice, and promoting peace. By living in harmony with ourselves and the world around us, we can help create a more just and peaceful world.

6. Morality

The sixth principle of Maat is morality. In Ancient Egyptian beliefs, the sixth principle of Maat emphasizes the importance of living a moral life. This principle encourages us to behave morally so that we can create a more just world for ourselves and future generations. This principle is reflected in the famous saying, "do unto others as you would have them do unto you." In other words, people should treat others with compassion and respect, just as they would want to be treated. This principle also includes the idea that people should avoid causing harm to others and that they should always seek to maintain a balanced and peaceful world.

This principle is represented by the Ankh of Maat, which symbolizes life and resurrection. In ancient Egypt, the ankh was often used as a symbol of power and authority. It is also a symbol of hope and renewal as it represents the cycle of life. This principle reminds us that our actions have consequences, both for ourselves and others. We must always strive to behave in a way that is morally right so that we can create a better world for all.

7. Respect

The seventh and final principle of Maat is respect. This includes respecting oneself, others, and the natural world. It also includes living in harmony with the divine order of the universe. This principle was closely linked to social status and reputation in ancient Egypt. Those who behaved properly were seen as being worthy of respect, while those who did not were viewed with suspicion and disdain. This principle is still relevant today. In a world where our actions are often viewed and judged by others, our behavior can have a lasting impact on our reputation. By behaving properly, we can show that we are respectful and trustworthy individuals.

This final principle is a call to action. It asks us to consider our words and actions carefully and to always strive to behave in a way that is respectful and proper. Many of the principles of Maat are interconnected, and this final principle reminds us that our actions have an impact on ourselves, others, and the world around us. We must always strive to behave in a way that is moral and just so that we can create a more peaceful and harmonious world.

Exercise

While the principles of Maat may seem simple, they provide a foundation for living a moral and just life. What do you think is the most important principle of Maat? Why? What does it mean to you? How can you apply it to your life?

To help you think about these questions, consider the following scenario:

You are at a party with friends when you see someone alone across the room who looks uncomfortable. You notice that the person is not drinking and appears to be looking for a way to leave. What do you do?

If you see someone alone at a party who looks uncomfortable, the best thing to do would be to go talk to them. Introduce yourself and try to make them feel more comfortable. Offer to get them a drink or food, and help them find a way to enjoy the party. The principles of Maat encourage us to always behave in a way that is respectful and compassionate. By talking to the person and trying to make them feel more comfortable, you are following the principle of propriety and helping to create a more harmonious world.

Whenever you come across a situation where you are not sure what the best thing to do is, ask yourself the following question:

- What is the impact of my actions on myself, others, and the world around me?
- How can I live in harmony with myself and the world around me?
- What does it mean to behave morally?
- What are some ways that I can respect others?

Asking yourself these questions can help you make the best decision possible in any given situation.

Relation between the Ten Commandments and the Principles of Maat

There are many similarities between the Ten Commandments and the Principles of Maat. Both systems of ethics emphasize the importance of truth, justice, and personal integrity. In addition, both sets of principles stress the importance of treating others with respect and compassion. However, there are also some key differences between the two systems. For example, while the Ten Commandments focus on preventing harm done to others, the Principles of Maat emphasize the need to actively help them. In addition, while the Ten Commandments are mainly concerned with earthly matters, the Principles of Maat also encompass spiritual principles. As a result, while both systems of ethics are very similar in many ways, they have some key differences.

The Principles of Maat provide a comprehensive ethical system that can be used to guide our behavior in both our personal and professional lives. Some of the key benefits of this system include the promotion of truth, justice, and personal integrity. In addition, the principles of Maat encourage us to treat others with respect and compassion. By following these principles, we can create a more peaceful and harmonious world for ourselves and future generations.

How the Laws of Maat Help One Pass into the Afterlife

The laws of Maat are closely connected to the Negative Confessions, a series of 42 statements that were recited by the dead during their journey through the underworld. The Negative Confessions served as a sort of moral compass for the dead, and they helped the gods determine whether or not the deceased had led a good life. The Assessors, which were a group of 42 gods, were responsible for judging the dead. Each god represented one of the 42 Laws of Maat, and they would determine whether or not the deceased had followed that particular law. If the deceased followed all 42 laws, they would be allowed to enter the afterlife. However, if they violated any of the laws, then they would be sent to the underworld, where they would be punished for their crimes.

The 42 Laws of Maat are a moral code that can help one live a good life. These laws encourage honesty, compassion, justice, and balance. If followed, these laws can help one avoid committing crimes and live in harmony with others. The laws of Maat can also help one achieve balance in their own life.

The 42 Laws of Maat are divided into seven categories, which are:
1. Maat, Truth, Justice, and Balance
2. Family, Marriage, and Children
3. Community and Country
4. Business and Work
5. Wealth and Property
6. Health and Well-Being
7. Spirituality and Religion

Each of these categories contains six laws, for a total of 42 laws. To achieve balance in one's life, it is important to follow all of the laws in each category. The laws guide how to live a good life and can help one avoid committing crimes. Furthermore, the laws can help one achieve balance in their own life.

The 42 Laws of Maat

The 42 Laws of Maat are a set of ancient Egyptian guidelines for living a good and virtuous life. The laws cover a wide range of topics, from honesty and justice to respect for elders and the environment. While some of the laws may seem outdated or irrelevant, many of them are still relevant today. For example, the law that states that one should not take what does not belong to them is just as relevant today as it was thousands of years ago. Likewise, the law that calls for treating others with respect is just as important today as it was in ancient times. By following the 42 Laws of Maat, we can live our lives by the values of an ancient and wise culture. Here are the 42 Laws of Maat:

1. I have not sinned.
2. I have not stolen.
3. I have not killed.
4. I have not lied.
5. I have not cheated.
6. I have not borne false witness against another.
7. I have not stolen food.
8. I have not committed adultery.
9. I have not coveted another's wife or husband.
10. I have not been disobedient.
11. I have not been rebellious.
12. I have not been dishonest.
13. I have not been deceitful.
14. I have not been vulgar.
15. I have not been impudent.
16. I have not been lazy.
17. I have done no wrong to the people around me.
18. I have not taken food from a child.
19. I have not deprived anyone of their rightful share of food.
20. I have not stolen bread.
21. I have not been greedy.
22. I have not stolen water.
23. I have neither wasted nor destroyed anything that has been given to me.
24. I have not spoken evil of another.
25. I have not raised my voice in anger.
26. I have not used abusive language.
27. I have refrained from cursing.
28. I have not behaved with arrogance.
29. I have not been deceitful or false in my speech.
30. I have not slandered or gossiped about others.
31. I have not been angry without just cause.
32. I have not avenged myself.

33. I have not inflicted punishment on another without just cause.
34. I have neither plotted evil against another nor wished them harm.
35. I have not insulted or humiliated another.
36. I have not behaved with violence or hatred.
37. I have not murdered or wished for the death of another.
38. I have neither oppressed nor persecuted others.
39. I have neither stolen from nor cheated another.
40. I have not forced anyone into sexual relations.
41. I have not taken part in or benefited from the enslavement of another.
42. I have neither plundered nor despoiled others' tombs or graves.

The 42 Laws of Maat are still relevant today as they provide us with a moral compass that can help us make good life choices. By following these laws, we can ensure that we live our lives by the values of an ancient and wise culture.

The Significance of the Number 42

The number 42 is significant in many cultures, including Egyptian, Greek, and Mayan. In Egyptian mythology, the gods represented by the 42 Laws of Maat were responsible for judging the dead. In Greek mythology, the number 42 was associated with the story of Oedipus, who killed his father and married his mother. In Mayan mythology, the gods created the world in 42 days.

The number 42 also has a significant role in mathematics and science. In mathematics, the number 42 is perfect, meaning that it is equal to the sum of its divisors. The number 42 is also unique, as it is the only number that is the product of two consecutive prime numbers. In science, the number 42 is the atomic number of molybdenum, a chemical element that is used in a variety of applications, including steel production.

In the Papyrus of Nebseni, which was written around 1350 BCE, there is a list of 42 negative confessions that the dead must recite to enter the afterlife. These confessions are very similar to the 42 Laws of Maat, and they serve as a reminder of the importance of living a good life.

The Papyrus of Ani is an ancient Egyptian funerary text that was written around 1240 BCE. In the papyrus, there is a statement that says, "Heaven lies in knowing Maat." The word "Maat" refers to truth, justice, and balance. It is also the name of the goddess who personifies these concepts.

The number 42 is often associated with this statement as it is the number of hieroglyphs that make up the word "Maat." Regardless of its meaning, the statement "Heaven lies in knowing Maat" is a powerful reminder of the importance of living a life based on truth, justice, and balance.

Laws and principles govern our lives, whether we realize it or not. There are basic laws that ensure public safety, and there are also moral principles that guide our behavior. The 42 Laws of Maat are an ancient Egyptian code of conduct that can help us live our lives by the values of a wise and ancient culture. By following these laws, we can ensure that we live our lives by the principles of truth, justice, and balance.

Chapter 4: Sacred Deities and How to Honor Them

Kemeticism is an ancient Egyptian religion that has been practiced for over 5,000 years. It is a polytheistic religion that recognizes the existence of many gods and goddesses. Maat is a central concept in Kemeticism, which is often described as the principle of truth, balance, order, harmony, law, and justice. Maat is represented by the goddess Maat, who was responsible for ensuring that the universe remains in balance.

The concept of Maat is closely linked to the gods and goddesses of Kemeticism as they are responsible for maintaining balance in the universe. This chapter will cover the three main deities of Kemeticism: Osiris, Isis, and Horus. We will also explore the role of Maat in Kemetism and how the gods and goddesses are connected to Maat. Finally, we will provide tips on how to connect with the deities and what offerings they prefer.

The Concept of Deities in Kemeticism

Kemeticism is a polytheistic religion that recognizes the existence of many gods and goddesses. The number of deities worshipped in Kemeticism varies depending on the particular tradition or sect. However, some deities are worshipped by most, if not all, Kemeticists. Kemeticism does not impose the worship of any specific deity. Instead, it is up to the individual to choose their desired deity, depending on their preference and beliefs.

The gods and goddesses of Kemeticism can be divided into two main categories, netjeru (gods) and netjetru (goddesses). Netjeru are typically associated with power, while netjetru are often associated with love and fertility. Netjeru are often depicted as animals, while netjetru are typically human. However, this is not always the case. For example, Isis is sometimes depicted as a bird or a cat, while Horus is sometimes depicted as a human. Let's take a closer look at Netjeru and Netjetru.

Netjeru

Netjeru are the gods of Kemetism. They are typically associated with power, strength, and virility. Netjeru are often considered to be the protectors of Kemetism and its followers. The term Netjeru comes from the Ancient Egyptian word ntr, which means god. The word ntr can also be translated to mean king, ruler, or lord. Some of the most popular Netjeru include:

- **Osiris:** The god of the underworld and the dead
- **Horus:** The god of the sky, sun, and war
- **Anubis:** The god of death and the underworld
- **Ptah:** The god of craftsmen and artisans

Netjetru

Netjetru are the goddesses of Kemetism. They are typically associated with love, fertility, and motherhood. Netjetru are often considered to be the caretakers of Kemetism and its followers. The term Netjetru comes from the Ancient Egyptian word ntrt, which means goddess. The word ntrt can also be translated to mean lady, queen, or ruler. Some of the most popular Netjetru include:

- **Isis:** The goddess of fertility, motherhood, and magic
- **Bast:** The goddess of cats, protection, and fertility
- **Hathor:** The goddess of love, beauty, and music
- **Sekhmet:** The goddess of war and destruction

Osiris

Osiris, god of the underworld and the dead.
Unknown authorUnknown author, CC0, via Wikimedia Commons:
https://commons.wikimedia.org/wiki/File:The_Sacred_Books_and_Early_Literature_of_the_East,_vol._2,_pg._64-65,_Osiris.jpg

In Kemeticism, Osiris is the god of the underworld and the dead. He is typically depicted as a green-skinned man with a Pharaoh's crown. He is often shown holding a staff or scepter. Osiris is the husband of Isis and the father of Horus. He is also the brother of Set. Osiris is also a god of fertility and agriculture. He is often depicted with green skin, which symbolizes new life and growth. Osiris is said to have created the Nile River, which was essential for the fertility of Ancient Egypt.

Worship

Osiris was very popular in Ancient Egypt. His cult began in the Predynastic Period and continued until the Roman period. His temple at

Abydos was one of the most important in Ancient Egypt. It was a pilgrimage site for Egyptians who wanted to honor their dead ancestors. Osiris was usually worshipped as part of a triad with Isis and Horus. However, he was also worshipped alone. His worship spread to other parts of the world, such as Greece and Rome.

Symbols and Correspondences
- **Color:** Green
- **Planet:** Mercury
- **Element:** Earth
- **Day of the week:** Wednesday
- **Number:** 4
- **Animal:** Bull
- **Plant:** Corn

Role in Kemeticism

Osiris is the lord of the underworld and judge of the dead in Ancient Egyptian mythology. He was killed by his brother, Set, who dismembered his body and scattered the pieces across Egypt. Isis, Osiris' wife, found the pieces and put them back together. With the help of Anubis, they embalmed Osiris' body and brought him back to life. Osiris then became the god of the underworld and the dead. He is often depicted as the protector of the deceased and the judge of the dead. In some myths, he is said to offer guidance and wisdom to the dead on their journey to the afterlife.

Tips on How to Connect with Osiris
- **Visit his Temple at Abydos:** This is one of the most important temples dedicated to Osiris. It is a pilgrimage site for many Kemetics.
- **Make Offerings:** Offerings can be made to Osiris on his feast day, which is celebrated on the fourth day of the month of Choiak. Offerings can include food, flowers, and incense.
- **Pray:** You can pray to Osiris for guidance, protection, and wisdom.
- **Meditate:** You can meditate on Osiris' myths and stories to learn more about him.
- **Make a Shrine:** You can create a shrine to Osiris in your home. It can be as simple or as elaborate as you like.

- **Write a Hymn:** You can write a hymn or poem in honor of Osiris.
- **Draw or Paint:** You can draw or paint Osiris. This is a way to connect with his creative side.
- **Dance:** You can dance in honor of Osiris. This is a way to connect with his energy and power.
- **Sing:** You can sing songs in honor of Osiris. This is a way to connect with his creative side.
- **Play Music:** Since he is the god of music, you can play music in honor of Osiris. This is a way to connect with his creative side.

Regardless of the method you choose to connect with Osiris, the most important thing is to be sincere in your desire to connect with him. The gods are more likely to respond to those who are sincere in their worship.

Isis

Isis, goddess of fertility, motherhood and magic.
Jeff Dahl, CC BYSA 4.0 <https://creativecommons.org/licenses/by-sa/4.0>, via Wikimedia Commons: https://commons.wikimedia.org/wiki/File:Isis.svg

Isis is the goddess of fertility, motherhood, and magic in Kemeticism. She is typically depicted as a woman with black skin and long hair. Isis is often shown wearing a headdress in the shape of a throne. She is the wife of Osiris and the mother of Horus. Isis is also a goddess of healing and protection.

Worship

Isis was very popular in Ancient Egypt. Her cult began in the Predynastic Period and continued until the Roman period. Her temple at Philae was one of the most important in Ancient Egypt. It was a pilgrimage site for Egyptians who wanted to honor their dead ancestors. Isis was usually worshipped as part of a triad with Osiris and Horus. However, she was also worshipped alone. Her worship spread to other parts of the world, such as Greece and Rome.

Symbols and Correspondences

- **Color:** Green
- **Planet:** Venus
- **Element:** Water
- **Day of the Week:** Friday
- **Number:** 7
- **Animal:** Cow
- **Plant:** Lotus

Role in Kemeticism

Isis is the goddess of fertility, motherhood, and magic in Kemeticism. She is the wife of Osiris and the mother of Horus. Isis is also a goddess of healing and protection. In some myths, she resurrected her husband, Osiris, after Set killed him. Isis is often depicted as a woman with black skin and long hair. She is usually shown wearing a headdress in the shape of a throne.

Tips on How to Connect with Isis

- **Visit her Temple at Philae:** This is one of the most important temples dedicated to Isis. It was a pilgrimage site for Egyptians who wanted to honor their dead ancestors.
- **Make Offerings:** Offerings can be made to Isis on her feast day, which is celebrated on the fifth day of the month of Choiak. Offerings can include food, flowers, and incense.

- **Pray:** You can pray to Isis for guidance, protection, and wisdom.
- **Meditate:** Meditation can be used to connect with Isis on a deeper level. Try meditating on her image or the banks of the Nile River.
- **Read About Her:** Read about Isis in mythology and history books. This will help you to understand her better.
- **Write About Her:** Writing about Isis can be a way to connect with her on a personal level. Write about your experiences, your prayers, and your offerings.
- **Create Art:** Creating art about Isis can be a way to connect with her. Draw, paint, or sculpt her image.
- **Wear Her Symbols:** Wearing the symbols of Isis can help you to feel closer to her. Common symbols include the ankh, the eye of Horus, and the lotus flower.
- **Make Music:** Making music dedicated to Isis can be a way to connect with her. You can sing, play instruments, or listen to music about her.
- **Dance:** Dancing is a way to connect with Isis on a physical level. Dance in honor of her and to the rhythm of her music.

With these tips, you can begin to connect with Isis and develop a relationship with this goddess. The most crucial thing is to be respectful and sincere in your actions. Show Isis that you are dedicated to her and want to learn more about her. As you do so, she will begin to reveal herself to you. Isis is a goddess who welcomes all who seek her. She is a loving and compassionate goddess who will guide you on your journey. Honor her, and she will honor you.

Horus

Horus, god of the sky, war, and hunting.
Jeff Dahl, CC BY SA 4.0 <https://creativecommons.org/licenses/by-sa/4.0>, via Wikimedia Commons: https://commons.wikimedia.org/wiki/File:Horus_standing.svg

Horus is the god of the sky, war, and hunting in Kemeticism. He is typically depicted as a man with the head of a falcon. Horus was the son of Isis and Osiris. He was also the brother of Set and Nephthys. In some myths, Horus fought against Set to avenge his father's death. In other myths, he was the judge of the dead in the underworld. Horus is often shown as a falcon-headed man or as a falcon. He is also sometimes depicted as a lion or a bull.

Worship of Horus

Horus was worshipped throughout Ancient Egypt. His cult center was at Edfu, where his temple is one of the best preserved in Egypt. Horus was also worshipped at Nekhen, where he was depicted as a falcon-headed man. He was also worshipped at Buto and Dendara. In the Roman period, Horus was syncretized with the god Apollo. The Greek form of his name is Horos.

Symbols and Correspondences

- **Color:** Red
- **Planet:** Mars
- **Element:** Fire
- **Day of the Week:** Tuesday
- **Number:** 4
- **Animal:** Falcon
- **Plant:** Wheat

Role in Kemeticism

Horus was one of the most important gods in ancient Egyptian religion. He was often depicted as a falcon or as a man with the head of a falcon. Horus was the god of the sky, and he was also associated with the sun, moon, and stars. He was often considered to be the protector of Egypt, and he was venerated as the patron god of kingship and victory. The ancient Egyptians believed that Horus would help them defeat their enemies and achieve success in their endeavors. In many ways, Horus served as a symbol of hope and strength for the Egyptian people.

Tips on How to Connect with Horus

- **Make Offerings:** Offerings can be made to Horus on his feast day, which is celebrated on the first day of the month of Thoth. Offerings can include food, drink, and incense.
- **Pray:** You can pray to Horus for guidance, protection, and strength.
- **Meditate:** Meditating on Horus's image can help you feel closer to him and better understand his energies.
- **Read About Him:** Reading about the deity you are trying to connect with is a great way to learn more about them. You can read myths, stories, or books about Egyptian religion and history to learn more about Horus.

- **Visit a Temple:** If you are lucky enough to live near an Egyptian temple or one that worships Horus, you can visit it and participate in the rituals and offerings there. This is a great way to connect with the energy of the deity.
- **Create Art:** You can create art in honor of Horus. This can be anything from painting and sculpture to music and dance.

By following these tips, you can begin to develop a relationship with Horus. No matter how you choose to connect with Horus, remember that he is a powerful and benevolent deity who can offer you guidance and strength.

Bast

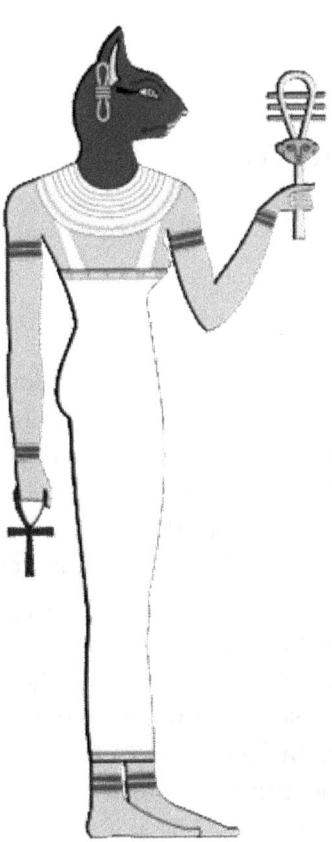

Bast, goddess of cats, protection, fertility and the home.
FDRMRZUSA, CC BYSA 4.0 <https://creativecommons.org/licenses/by-sa/4.0>, via Wikimedia Commons: https://commons.wikimedia.org/wiki/File:Bastet_mirror.svg

Bast is the goddess of cats, protection, fertility, and the home in Kemeticism. She is typically depicted as a woman with the head of a cat or a lioness. Bast was the daughter of Ra and Isis. She was also the sister of Horus and Set. In some myths, Bast protected Ra from the serpent Apep. In other myths, she was the goddess of the home and hearth. She is also sometimes depicted as a cow or a snake.

Worship of Bast

Bast was worshipped throughout Ancient Egypt. Her cult center was at Bubastis, where her temple was one of the largest and most elaborate in Egypt. Bast was also worshipped at Sekhmet, where she was depicted as a lioness. In the Roman period, Bast was syncretized with the goddess Diana.

Symbols and Correspondences

- **Color:** Red
- **Planet:** Mars
- **Element:** Fire
- **Day of the Week:** Tuesday
- **Number:** 9
- **Animal:** Cat
- **Plant:** Wheat

Role in Kemeticism

In Kemeticism, Bast is the goddess of cats, fertility, dance, and music. She is also known as the Lady of the East and is associated with the sun god Ra. As a cat goddess, Bast is often depicted as a black cat or a lioness. She is occasionally shown as a woman with a cat's head or as a cat with a woman's head. In her role as a fertility goddess, Bast is responsible for providing food and clothing for the people of Egypt.

She was also believed to protect women during childbirth and to assist them in their journey to the afterlife. As a goddess of dance and music, Bast was thought to bring joy and pleasure to those who worshipped her. In addition to her many roles, Bast was also considered to be a protector of the home and family. In Kemeticism, Bast is honored for her many qualities and her ability to bring happiness and abundance to those who worship her.

Tips on How to Connect with Bast

- **Make Offerings:** Offerings can be made to Bast on her feast day, which is celebrated on the fifth day of the month of Hathor. Offerings can include food, drink, and incense.
- **Pray:** You can pray to Bast for guidance, protection, fertility, and abundance.
- **Make Art:** Draw, paint, or sculpt images of Bast. Create altars or shrines dedicated to her.
- **Dance:** Dance is a form of prayer and can be used to raise energy and connect with the goddess.
- **Write:** Write stories, poems, or songs about Bast.
- **Meditate:** Bast is a solar goddess, and you can meditate on her image to connect with her energy.
- **Celebrate:** Celebrate Bast's feast day by holding a small ceremony in her honor. You can light candles, say prayers, and make offerings.

Bast is a fierce and powerful goddess who can offer her devotees guidance, protection, and abundance. If you are seeking a connection with Bast, these tips can help you get started.

Hathor

Hathor, goddess of love, beauty, fertility, music and dance.
https://commons.wikimedia.org/wiki/File:Hathor-Meyers.png

Hathor is the goddess of love, beauty, fertility, music, and dance in Kemeticism. She is typically depicted as a woman with a cow's head or as a cow. Hathor was the daughter of Ra and Isis. She was also the sister of Horus and Set. In some myths, Hathor is the mother of Horus. In other myths, she is the lover of Set. Hathor is associated with the planet Venus.

Worship of Hathor

Hathor was worshipped throughout Ancient Egypt. Her cult centers were at Dendera and Philae. Hathor was also worshipped at Sekhmet, where she was depicted as a lioness. In the Roman period, she was a goddess of love and pleasure, and her cult was popular among both men and women. The worship of Hathor was particularly important in the city of Dendera, where her temple was one of the largest and most magnificent in all of Egypt. Today, Hathor is still revered by many people, and her image can be seen in artwork, jewelry, and statues throughout the world.

Symbols and Correspondences

- **Color:** Green
- **Planet:** Venus
- **Element:** Earth
- **Day of the Week:** Friday
- **Number:** 7
- **Animal:** Cow
- **Plant:** Lotus

Role in Kemeticism

Hathor was a major goddess in Ancient Egyptian religion, and she played an important role in Kemeticism, the religious beliefs and practices of the Kemetic people. Hathor was usually depicted as a cow or a woman with the head of a cow, and she was associated with fertility, motherhood, love, music, and dance.

Hathor was associated with the sun god Ra, and she was sometimes said to be his daughter. She was also linked to the goddess Isis and was sometimes said to be Isis' sister. Hathor was worshiped throughout Egypt, and her cult center was at Dendera. Kemeticists often honor Hathor through music, dance, and other creative activities.

Tips to Connect with Hathor

- **Make Offerings:** Offerings can be made to Hathor on her feast day, which is celebrated on the 15th day of the month of Hathor.

Offerings can include flowers, incense, and milk.
- **Write a Hymn:** A hymn to Hathor can be written and recited as part of your daily devotionals.
- **Create Art:** Drawing or painting images of Hathor can be a form of devotional practice.
- **Dance:** Hathor is associated with music and dance, so incorporating these into your devotional practice can be a way to connect with her.
- **Wear Her Symbols:** Wearing jewelry or amulets that depict Hathor's symbols can help you to feel closer to her.

Hathor is a goddess who can be honored in many ways. If you want to connect with her, consider making offerings, writing a hymn, creating art, dancing, or wearing her symbols. By incorporating these activities into your devotional practice, you can create a strong connection with Hathor.

One of the great things about Kemeticism is that it does not impose the worship of any specific deity. This means that you can choose to focus your worship on whichever god or goddess you feel most connected to. Whether you prefer the radiant sun god Ra, the powerful lioness Bast, or the sage protector Thoth, there is a place for you in the Kemetic pantheon. And because Kemeticism is not dogmatic, you are free to change your focus as your spiritual needs evolve. As a result, Kemeticism provides a flexible and inclusive approach to spirituality that can be adapted to meet your changing needs.

The sacred deities of ancient Egypt were, and still are, very important to the people who honored them. They provide a connection to the divine and can offer guidance and protection. If you seek to connect with ancient Egypt's sacred deities, consider doing so through offering, writing hymns, creating art, dancing, or wearing their symbols. By incorporating these into your devotional practice, you can connect strongly with ancient Egypt's sacred deities.

Chapter 5: Honoring Akhu, Our Ancestors

Ancestor veneration is an important part of Ancient Egyptian spirituality and many other African spiritual traditions. The term "Akhu" refers to the Ancient Egyptian ancestors, and they are honored for their connection to the gods, as well as their wisdom, strength, protection, love, compassion, inspiration, hope, joy, pride, cultural identity, and spiritual identity. There are many ways to honor the Akhu, and some of the most popular methods include offering them food and drink, lighting candles or incense for them, and writing their names in spiritual books. This chapter will explore the concept of Akhu, why they are important, and how to give them offerings.

Akhu - The Ancient Egyptian Ancestors

The Akhu were the ancient Egyptian ancestors who were thought to live in the Duat, the underworld. The Akhu were often represented as birds or falcons, and their name means "those who are of the light." According to Egyptian belief, the Akhu were responsible for guiding the sun god Ra through the Duat each night, and they also helped Osiris, the god of the dead, judge the souls of the deceased.

The Akhu were also associated with Horus, the god of kingship, and they were sometimes said to be his eyes. In many ways, the Akhu represented everything good and pure in Egyptian society and were greatly revered by the people. With such an important role in Egyptian culture, it is no surprise that the Akhu were thought to be powerful beings who could intercede on behalf of humans in the afterlife.

The Akhu were often invoked in spells and prayers, and offerings were made to them in hopes that they would grant favor to the living. The Akhu were also thought to be able to protect against evil forces, and amulets bearing their image were worn for this purpose.

Why Are the Akhu Important?

The Akhu were important for many reasons, and they played a vital role in Ancient Egyptian spirituality. Here are some of the most important reasons the Akhu were such an integral part of Kemetic belief:

Our Link to the Gods

In ancient Egyptian belief, the Akhu were the spirits of the deceased who had passed on to the afterlife. They were also known as the "shining ones" or the "blessed dead." The Akhu were thought to dwell in the Duat, the realm of the dead, and had the power to intervene in the affairs of the living. They could be invoked for help and guidance and are often depicted as birds or animals.

The Akhu were also believed to be our link to the gods. They could carry our prayers and petitions to the gods, and they could intercede on our behalf. In this way, they became our protectors and allies. Today, we still revere the Akhu as our close companions in life and death. We believe they are always with us, watching over us and guiding us on our journey through this world.

The Akhu as a Source of Wisdom and Guidance

The Akhu are the spirits of the dead who have not been able to move on to the afterlife. As they are believed to know about both the living and the dead, they are often consulted for their wisdom and guidance. The Akhu play an important role in many cultures, providing comfort and support to the bereaved and helping to guide the living through difficult times.

In some traditions, the Akhu are also seen as protectors, and it is said that they can watch over us from the other side. Whether you believe in them or not, there is no denying that the Akhu offer a unique perspective on life and death. And for those who are grieving, they can provide much-needed solace and support.

The Akhu as a Source of Strength and Protection

The Akhu are the spirits of one's ancestors who have passed on to the afterlife. They are a source of strength and protection and can be called upon for help in times of need. The Akhu are also believed to be protectors of the living, and they can be invoked to help ward off evil forces. In some cultures, the Akhu are also seen as healers, and it is said that they can help to cure the sick. Whether you believe in them or not, there is no denying that the Akhu are a powerful force in the spiritual realm. And for those who are looking for strength and protection, they can be valuable allies.

The Akhu as a Source of Love and Compassion

The Akhu, or "soul" in ancient Egyptian, is often associated with love and compassion. The Akhu is often seen as the source of these emotions and other positive qualities such as loyalty and faithfulness. This connection is because the Akhu are seen as immortal and eternal beings. As such, it is believed that the Akhu have a deep understanding of love and compassion.

Akhu helps people find their way back to the light.
https://unsplash.com/photos/5B8Pw-t9_Wo?utm_source=unsplash&utm_medium=referral&utm_content=creditShareLink

In addition, it is believed that the Akhu can help us navigate life's challenges and find our way back to the light. For this reason, many people turn to the Akhu for guidance and support during difficult times.

While the Akhu are often associated with love and compassion, they are also a powerful force for good. By turning to the Akhu for guidance, we can tap into their power to overcome challenges and bring more love and compassion into our lives.

The Akhu as a Source of Inspiration

Every day, we are surrounded by countless sources of inspiration. For some, it may be the beauty of nature, while for others, it may be a work of art or a loved one. However, there is one source of inspiration that is often overlooked, the Akhu. In many cultures, the Akhu are honored and respected, and their guidance is sought out in times of need. For those who believe in them, the Akhu are a powerful source of inspiration.

They inspire us in many ways. They can offer advice and guidance when we are facing difficult decisions. They can give us strength when we are feeling lost or alone. And they can help us to see the beauty in life, even in the darkest of times. When we open ourselves up to their influence, the Akhu can help us find hope and meaning in our lives. So next time you are feeling lost or confused, remember to look to the Akhu for inspiration. Their guidance can help you find your way back to peace and happiness.

The Akhu as a Source of Hope

They are a powerful symbol of hope for the people of Ghana. For centuries, the idea of Akhu has been passed down from generation to generation, serving as a reminder of the strength and resilience of the Ghanaian people. The Akhu represent the unbreakable bond between the living and the dead, and it is believed that they have the power to protect against evil spirits.

In times of trouble, the Akhu are a reminder that our ancestors are always with us, watching over us and providing us with guidance. It is a symbol of hope that no matter what challenges we face, we will always be able to overcome them. The Akhu are more than just a part of mythology, they are a powerful reminder of who we are and what we are capable of.

The Akhu as a Source of Joy

The Akhu are often seen as a source of joy and happiness. In many cultures, the Akhu are honored and respected for their ability to bring happiness into our lives. It is believed that the Akhu have the power to make us laugh when we are feeling down and help us see the beauty in life.

The Akhu remind us that even in the darkest of times, there is always something to be thankful for. When we open ourselves up to Akhu's influence, we can find joy and happiness in the simplest things. So next time you are feeling down, remember to look to the Akhu for a little bit of joy. Their presence in your life can make all the difference.

The Akhu as a Source of Pride

The Akhu are a source of pride for many people. They have a long and rich history and are known for their beautiful artwork and stunning jewelry. They are also known for their friendly nature, and they are always quick to help those in need. In addition, they are known for their love of nature, and they often go on hikes and camping trips. The Akhu are a proud people who will always be an important part of our world.

The Akhu as a Source of Cultural Identity

In popular culture, the Akhu are often depicted as shining stars or burning lamps. For many people, they represent a powerful source of cultural identity. In a world that is constantly changing, they provide a connection to the past and a sense of stability. For Egyptians, the Akhu are a reminder of their rich culture and history. They offer comfort and hope in times of trouble and bring joy in times of happiness. They are an important part of who we are, and we will always be proud to call them our own.

The Akhu as a Source of Spiritual Identity

In many cultures, the Akhu are seen as a source of spiritual identity. For many people, the Akhu are a reminder of their connection to the divine. In Kemetic spirituality, they are often seen as an intermediary between the living and the dead. They are believed to have the power to guide us on our journey through life and help us find our way back to the gods. The Akhu are a powerful reminder of our spiritual identity and can help us connect with the divine in times of need. For these reasons, the Akhu are essential to many people's spiritual lives.

Ways to Honor the Akhu

The Akhu are honored in many cultures around the world. In Ancient Egypt, they were known as the "Glorious Dead" and were revered as protectors of the living. They are known as "Dewa" in Tibet and are believed to be powerful guardians of the Dharma. In Japan, they are known as "Kami" and are honored as the spirits of nature. There are many ways to honor the Akhu, but some common methods include offerings of food and drink, lighting candles or lamps, and reciting prayers or mantras. By honoring them, we ensure that their beneficial influence will continue to be felt in our lives.

1. Offerings

To honor the Akhu and ensure their goodwill, offerings were often made to them. These offerings could take the form of food, drink, or even items that the Akhu might find useful in the afterlife. The most important thing was that the offering was given with sincere respect and a desire to please the spirits. The Akhu were thought to be able to influence the lives of the living, so it was important to appease them.

Offerings were usually made at funerals, but they could also be given at other times, such as when someone was starting a new business or going on a dangerous journey. By making an offering to the Akhu, one was asking for their protection and guidance. In return, it was believed that the Akhu would bestow blessings upon those who honored them.

2. Prayers

The Akhu are honored through prayer in many different cultures. Prayer is one way to show our respect for the Akhu, and it can also be used to request their help and guidance. There are many different prayers to honor the Akhu, and each culture has its unique way of expressing this respect. However, all of these prayers share a common goal, to show our ancestors that we are grateful for their guidance and that we will always remember them.

3. Rituals

In ancient Egyptian belief, families would perform rituals to honor their ancestors and to ensure that their Akhu would be able to guide and protect them from the perils of the underworld. One such ritual was the "Opening of the Mouth" ceremony, in which a priest would touch the mouth of a mummy with an adze, a sacred tool used to break open the mouth. This would supposedly allow the spirit of the deceased to speak and be heard in the Land of the Dead.

Other rituals included offering food and drink to the Akhu, as well as reciting spells and performing dances. Although these practices might seem strange to us today, they served an important purpose for the ancient Egyptians. They believed they could ensure their place in the afterlife by honoring their ancestors.

4. Festivals

Festivals to honor the Akhu or ancestors are a common tradition in many cultures around the world. These festivals are a way to remember and show respect for those who have come before us. They can be somber affairs, or they can be joyous celebrations. Often, they involve special foods and drinks, as well as music and dance. Ancestor veneration is not just about honoring the dead. It is also about connecting with our heritage and keeping the stories and traditions of our culture alive.

For many people, these festivals are an important part of their identity and offer a chance to come together with others who share that identity. So, whether you are attending an Akhu festival or simply honoring your ancestors, take a moment to appreciate the importance of this time-honored tradition.

5. Cemeteries

In many cultures, the afterlife is a key belief, and many rituals and traditions surround death. One of these traditions is the proper care of the Akhu or ancestors. The Akhu are believed to be able to help those still living, but they must be properly honored and taken care of to do so. One way to do this is through cemetery care. Cemeteries are not only a place to bury the dead but also a place to honor them.

By keeping the cemetery clean and well-tended, we honor our ancestors and show them that we still remember them. In addition, many cemeteries have special days or times when members of the community can come together to perform rituals or make offerings. This is a time to give thanks for Akhu's help and ask for their continued guidance. By taking care of our cemeteries, we ensure that the Akhu are properly honored and can continue to help us in our lives.

6. Ancestor Altars

In many cultures around the world, it is customary to honor one's ancestors. In Egypt, this was done through lavish tombs and temples built to house the bodies and spirits of the dead. In China, the practice of ancestor worship helped to ensure that the deceased would be taken care of in the afterlife. Today, many people still maintain ancestor altars as a way to connect with their departed loved ones.

For those of Egyptian descent, ancestor altars are often decorated with images of Anubis, the god of the dead. Offerings of food and drink are also left out for the ancestors, and special prayers are said to honor their memory. The Akhu, or spirits of the dead, are also venerated in many

African cultures. Ancestor altars play an important role in maintaining a connection to one's heritage and ensuring that the past is never forgotten.

7. Genealogies

The Akhu are the spirits of our ancestors, and they play an important role in Egyptian culture. Genealogies were used to honor them and keep their memory alive. They were also used to help people connect with their past and understand their place in the world. Genealogies were often carved into stone or painted on walls. They listed the names of Pharaohs, nobles, and other important people. They also told stories about famous events. We can learn a lot about ancient Egyptian history by studying these records. Genealogies are an essential part of our heritage, and they help us to connect with our past.

8. Stories

In many traditions, it is believed that the Akhu can help us connect with our deceased loved ones and receive guidance from them. For this reason, many people choose to honor the Akhu through story-telling. By sharing stories about our ancestors, we keep their memories alive and allow their wisdom to live on. In addition, telling stories about the Akhu can be a way of showing respect for their tremendous impact on our lives. Whether we share personal anecdotes or traditional folktales, stories about the Akhu help strengthen our connection to them.

9. Art

For the ancient Egyptians, death was not the end. They believed in an afterlife and that their Akhu, or spirit, would live on. As a result, they took great care to prepare for the journey and to honor their Akhu through art. One of the most common ways to do this was to create funerary masks. These masks were made from a variety of materials, including wood, stone, and gold. They were often highly decorated, with paintings and hieroglyphs that conveyed messages of hope and protection.

Funerary masks served both practical and spiritual purposes. They helped preserve the body of the deceased and also helped guide the Akhu on their journey to the afterlife. Today, Egyptian funerary masks are some of the world's most iconic pieces of art. They serve as a reminder of the Egyptians' beliefs and of their commitment to honoring their dead.

10. Music

One way to honor the Akhu is through music. The Akhu are often depicted as birds, so many songs make use of bird calls to summon their presence. Other songs make use of percussion to create a feeling of movement as if the Akhu are dancing. Still, others make use of chanting and wordless vocalizations to create an ethereal atmosphere in which the Akhu can move freely. No matter what style of music is used, it is clear that music played an important role in Ancient Egyptian belief.

What and How to Give Offerings to the Akhu

The Akhu are the spirits of one's ancestors and play an important role in Ancient Egyptian religion. Offerings were given to the Akhu to ensure their continued support and protection. The most common offerings included food, drink, and mummified remains. Food offerings were usually placed on a table in the tomb or shrine, and drink offerings were poured into jars that were buried in the ground. Mummified offerings were usually placed in coffins or stelae. The Akhu were also thought to be able to accept non-physical offerings, such as prayers and hymns. In general, it was believed that the more elaborate the offering, the more likely it was to be accepted by the Akhu.

When giving offerings to the Akhu, it is crucial to be respectful. One should always approach the Akhu with clean hands and a pure heart. It is also vital to give thanks for Akhu's guidance and protection. Offerings should be given regularly, not just when one needs help. By regularly honoring the Akhu, we show our appreciation for all that they have done for us.

Worshiping and honoring the Akhu is an important part of Ancient Egyptian religion. It is a way to connect with one's ancestors and receive their guidance. Many ways to honor the Akhu include story-telling, music, and giving offerings. The most important thing is to approach the Akhu with respect and gratitude. By doing so, we ensure that our connection to them remains strong.

Chapter 6: Building a Shrine

Personal shrines are a great way to connect with the deities and ancestors you hold dear. By creating a space that is dedicated to them, you can create a place of worship and connection that is entirely your own. Not only that, but personal shrines can also be incredibly helpful in times of need or struggle. By having a space that is specifically devoted to the divine, you can go to them for guidance, strength, and solace whenever you need it.

Building a shrine is a very personal process, and there is no one right way to do it. However, there are some general guidelines that can be followed to create a space that is both sacred and safe. In this chapter, we will go over some of the basics of shrine-building, including how to select a location, what kind of objects to include, and how to care for your shrine. By the end, you'll have everything you need to create a personal space that is perfect for you and your practice.

Personal Shrines/Altars

A personal shrine is a space that is dedicated to the worship of specific deities or ancestors. It can be as simple as a small shelf with a few statues and offerings or as elaborate as an entire room filled with objects and rituals. Shrines can be temporary or permanent, indoors or outdoors, and can be created for any deity or ancestor that you wish to honor.

There are many reasons why someone might create a personal shrine. For some, it is a way to connect with specific deities daily. For others, it is a way to create a space for reflection and contemplation. And for others still, it is a way to cultivate a sense of peace and calm in their everyday lives. No matter what your reasons are, creating a personal shrine can be a very rewarding experience.

How Shrines Are Used

Shrines are a common sight in many cultures around the world. They can be used for various purposes, from honoring ancestors to protection from evil spirits. Often, shrines are built to commemorate special events or people. For example, shrines dedicated to the owners of successful businesses are often found in Japanese neighborhoods.

Shrines can also be used as a way to mark significant changes in one's life. In some cultures, a shrine is erected when a child is born and added to as the child grows older. Shrines can be simple or elaborate, but they all serve as a reminder of the things that are important to us.

There are many ways to use a personal shrine. Some people use them as a way to connect with specific deities daily, while others only visit them for special occasions or holidays. Shrines can also be used as a space for reflection and contemplation or as a place to offer up prayers and petitions.

The most important thing is to find a way to use your shrine that works for you. There is no wrong way to use a personal shrine, so long as it brings you closer to the divine. The following are some ideas to get you started:

1. Use your shrine as a way to connect with specific deities daily. This can be done by offering up prayers, offerings, or simply spending time in their presence.
2. Use your shrine as a space for reflection and contemplation. This can be done by spending time meditating in front of your shrine or by using it as a place to journal about your spiritual journey.
3. Use your shrine as a place to offer up prayers and petitions. This can be done by writing down your requests and placing them in front of your shrine or by saying them out loud while you are in front of your shrine.
4. Use your shrine as a way to cultivate a sense of peace and calm in your everyday life. This can be done by spending time in front of your shrine each day or by using it as a place to retreat when you need a moment of peace.

5. Use your shrine as a way to connect with your ancestors. This can be done either by placing photos or objects that belonged to them in front of your shrine or by offering prayers and libations to them.

Building a Shrine: Step-by-Step Instructions

If you're interested in building your shrine, the following are some simple instructions to get you started.

1. Selecting Location

When choosing a location for your shrine, there are a few things to keep in mind. First, consider the purpose of the shrine. What do you want to use it for? Will you be using it for daily worship or only on special occasions? If you plan on using it regularly, you'll want to choose an easily accessible spot.

A spot near the front door or in your bedroom might be ideal. However, suppose you only plan on using it occasionally. In that case, you may want to choose a more hidden location, such as in the back of your closet or under the stairs. Second, think about who will be using the shrine. If you are the only one who will be accessing it, then you have more flexibility in terms of its location. However, if others will be using it, you'll need to choose a spot that is large enough to accommodate them comfortably.

Third, consider your personal preferences. What kind of atmosphere do you want to create? Do you prefer a more private or open and inviting setting? Once you have considered these factors, you should better know where to locate your shrine.

2. Choosing Deities/Ancestors to Represent

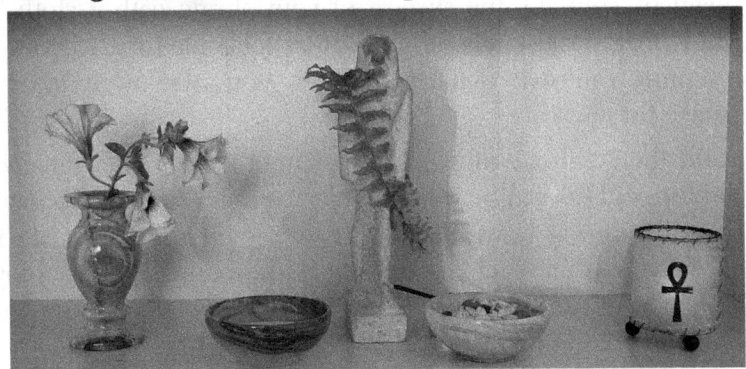

Altar for the god Thoth.,
https://commons.wikimedia.org/wiki/File:Th_oltar.JPG

One of the most important aspects of building a personal shrine is deciding which deities or ancestors you want to represent. If you're unsure where to start, consider your spiritual beliefs and traditions. Are there any specific deities that you feel drawn to? Alternatively, you may want to choose deities or ancestors that have meaning in your family history.

Once you've decided on one or more deities or ancestors to represent, do some research to learn more about them. What are their symbols and colors? What kinds of offerings do they enjoy? What are their stories and myths? The more you know about the beings you are representing, the easier it will be to create a shrine that feels like a sacred space.

3. Gather Materials

Now that you know where your shrine will be located and which deities/ancestors you want to represent, it's time to gather the materials that you'll need to create it.

- A small table, altar, or shelf on which to place your shrine items
- A cloth to cover the surface of your shrine. This can be anything from a simple piece of fabric to a more elaborate altar cloth
- Images or statues of the deities/ancestors you are representing
- Symbolic items that represent each deity/ancestor. Some examples are flowers for a goddess of love, a candle for a god of fire, or a bowl of water for a goddess of the sea.
- Offerings for the deities/ancestors. Tese can include food, drink, flowers, incense, or anything else you feel called to offer.

4. Assemble Your Shrine

Once you have all of your materials, it's time to start assembling your shrine. Begin by covering the surface of your shrine with a cloth. Then, arrange your images or statues in a way that feels pleasing to you. If you are representing multiple deities/ancestors, you may want to create a separate space for each one.

Next, add the symbolic items that represent each being. Finally, offer up your offerings. This can be done by placing them directly on the shrine or by using an offering bowl. The most important thing is to do it with intention. As you offer each item, take a moment to say a prayer or visualization. For example, you might imagine the deity/ancestor receiving your offering and being pleased.

5. Bless Your Shrine

Once your shrine is assembled, you'll want to bless it to make it a sacred space. Depending on your personal preferences, this can be done in any number of ways. Cleanse it thoroughly with salt water or sand. Once it's clean, you're ready to consecrate it. To do this, light a white candle and some incense, and then say a prayer – asking for the blessing of the gods or goddesses you wish to honor.

You can also anoint your shrine with oil, using a circular motion to infuse it with positive energy. Once your shrine is consecrated, you can begin to decorate it with images or statues of the deities you wish to honor. You can also add fresh flowers or other offerings that are dear to them. Remember, your shrine is a sacred space where you can go to connect with the divine. Treat it with respect and care, and it will serve as a powerful source of strength and guidance in your life.

Place and Placement of Objects on the Shrine

The arrangement of objects on a shrine is usually quite deliberate and can have a deep significance. In many cases, the placement of objects is dictated by tradition or religious beliefs. For example, many shrines will have a statue or picture of a deity in the center, surrounded by offerings or symbols of veneration. The specific items included in a shrine can also vary depending on the purpose of the shrine. For instance, a shrine dedicated to an ancestor might include items that were important to that person in life, such as photos or mementos. Ultimately, the placement of objects on a shrine often reflects the relationship between the worshipper and the object of worship.

1. Statues or Images of Deities

The most common type of object found on a shrine is some form of statue or image of the deity being worshipped. This could be anything from a small figurine to a large painting or sculpture. As it is seen as the focal point, the statue or image is usually placed in the center of the shrine. The statue or image is the worshipper's main object in many cases.

2. Offerings

Offerings are another common type of object found on shrines and can be anything the worshipper wants to offer up to the deity, such as food, drink, flowers, incense, or even armor in some cases. The offering is usually placed in front of the statue or the deity's image to show respect and devotion.

3. Symbolic Items

In some cases, shrines will also include symbolic items that represent the deity being worshipped. This could be anything from a specific type of flower to a certain kind of stone or metal. Including these items is usually meant to help the worshipper connect with the deity on a more personal level.

4. Photos or Mementos

Another type of object often found on shrines is photos or mementos of the person or thing being worshipped. This is particularly common in shrines dedicated to ancestors, as it helps create a more personal connection. As they are seen as secondary to the main statue or image, these items are usually placed around the periphery of the shrine.

5. Fresh Flowers

Fresh flowers are often used to decorate shrines as they are seen as a symbol of life and growth. They also have a pleasant smell that can help create a more relaxing and inviting atmosphere. The flowers are usually placed around the outside of the shrine to frame the central image or statue.

6. Incense

Incense is another common type of offering that is often used to decorate shrines. It is seen as a way of purifying the space and creating a more holy atmosphere. The incense is usually placed in front of the shrine to waft the smoke towards the central image or statue. Be careful when burning incense, as it can be a fire hazard.

7. Candles

Candles are often used on shrines to create light and warmth. They can also be used to represent the presence of the divine. The candles are usually placed around the outside of the shrine to frame the central image or statue. Due to the fire hazard, make sure to be careful when using candles.

8. Bells

Bells are sometimes used on shrines as a way of calling attention to the presence of the divine. They can also be used to ward off evil spirits. The bells are usually hung outside the shrine to frame the central image or statue. The ringing of the bell can also be used to signal the start of a worship service.

9. Offerings Bowl

An offering bowl is sometimes used on shrines to collect offerings for the deity. The bowl is usually placed in front of the shrine to catch any offerings that are made. The bowl can also be used to hold water for cleansing rituals. With proper care, an offering bowl can last for many years.

10. Other Objects

Shrines can also include other objects that are specific to the deity being worshipped or the culture of the worshippers. This could be anything from weapons to musical instruments. Including these objects is usually meant to help the worshipper connect with the deity on a more personal level.

Remember, the placement of objects on a shrine is often quite deliberate and can have a deep significance. Make sure to take some time to consider the arrangement of items on your shrine to create a space that is meaningful to you.

Care and Maintenance of the Shrine

Proper care and maintenance of the shrine are essential for ensuring that it remains a place of worship for future generations. The first step in shrine maintenance is regularly cleaning the floors and surfaces. This helps remove dirt, dust, and other debris accumulated over time.

In addition, it is crucial to regularly inspect the shrine for any damage or wear. If any cracks or chips are found, they should be repaired immediately. Furthermore, the shrine should be watered regularly to keep the wood from drying out and cracking. By following these simple tips, you can ensure that the shrine remains a beautiful and sacred place of worship for years to come.

1. Daily Care

Every day, the shrine's priests perform a series of rituals to prepare the shrine for the day ahead. These rituals include cleansing the altar with salt water, burning incense, and making offerings of food and drink. In addition, the priests chant hymns and prayers to purify the shrine and call upon the ancestors' spirits. Once the shrine has been prepared, it is open to visitors who come to offer prayers and gifts.

The priests are responsible for ensuring that the shrine is kept clean and tidy, and they also guide those who seek advice from the spirits of the ancestors. By performing these daily rituals, the priests maintain the connection between the living and the dead and ensure that the ancestors can continue to guide and protect their descendants.

Here are some tips for the daily care of your shrine:
- Regularly clean the floors and surfaces of the shrine
- Inspect the shrine for any damage or wear
- Water the shrine regularly to keep the wood from drying out and cracking
- Dust the shrine regularly to remove any accumulation of dust and debris
- Offer food, drink, and incense to the spirits of the ancestors daily

2. Weekly Care

In addition to the daily care of the shrine, it is also necessary to perform a series of weekly rituals. These rituals include cleaning the statue or image of the deity, polishing the altar, and changing the offerings. The weekly care of the shrine helps to ensure that the shrine remains clean and sacred.

Here are some tips for the weekly care of your shrine:
- Clean the statue or image of the deity with a soft cloth
- Polish the altar with a clean, dry cloth
- Change the offerings on the altar to fresh food and drink
- Incense the shrine with quality incense
- Chant hymns and prayers to the spirits of the ancestors

3. Seasonal Care

The shrine also needs to be taken care of on a seasonal basis. This includes cleaning the shrine, changing the offerings, and performing rituals specific to the season. This care ensures that the shrine remains sacred and connected to the cycles of nature.

Here are some tips for the seasonal care of your shrine:
- Clean the shrine thoroughly at the start of each season
- Change the offerings on the altar to reflect the season
- Incense the shrine with seasonal incense
- Chant hymns and prayers that are specific to the season
- Perform rituals that are specific to the season

4. Annual Care

In addition to the shrine's daily, weekly, and seasonal care, it is also necessary to perform a series of annual rituals. These rituals include cleansing the shrine, offering offerings to the ancestors' spirits, and holding festivals. The annual care of the shrine helps to ensure that the shrine remains a sacred place of worship for years to come.

Here are some tips for the annual care of your shrine:
- Cleanse the shrine with salt water at the start of the year
- Make offerings of food, drink, and incense to the spirits of the ancestors
- Hold festivals and celebrations at the shrine throughout the year
- Invite the community to participate in the care of the shrine

5. Other Considerations

There are a few other things to remember when caring for your shrine. First, it is important to create a space that is sacred and safe. This means that the shrine should be located where outside influences will not disturb it. Second, it is important to respect the ancestors' shrines and spirits. This means that only those who are sincere in their desire to worship should be allowed to enter or visit. Finally, remember that the shrine is a living space and should be treated as such. This means that the shrine should be kept clean and free of clutter.

In Kemetism, the shrine is seen as a sacred space where one can go to connect with the divine. It is also seen as a place of protection and healing. The objects placed on the shrine are meant to help the worshipper connect with the deity and create a more holy and inviting atmosphere. With proper care, a shrine can last for many years. So, if you are interested in building your own Kemetism shrine, follow the tips outlined in this chapter.

Chapter 7: Maat and Magick

Maat Magick is a relatively new concept brought forward by occultist Nema Andahadna. It is a Thelemic system of self-initiation based on Aleister Crowley's writings. In this chapter, we will briefly touch upon what Maat Magick is, how it compares and differs from other systems of magick, and some of its key concepts.

What Is Maat Magick?

Nema Andahadna, an occultist, introduced the idea of Maat Magick. Maat Magick is a system of self-initiation based on Aleister Crowley's writings. It is named after the Egyptian goddess Maat, who represents truth, balance, and justice. The main goal of Maat Magick is to achieve balance in one's life and to live by the Law of Return.

Andahadna believes that by aligning oneself with the energy of Maat, one can create positive change in the world. To do this, she has created a system of rituals and practices designed to promote truth, justice, and balance in all areas of life. This includes both personal and global issues.

Andahadna found that by working with the energies of Maat, she could create positive change in her own life and in the lives of those around her. In addition, she believes that this type of magick can be used to help heal the planet and create a more peaceful and harmonious world.

Thelema and Thelemic Magick

Founded by Aleister Crowley in the early 20th century, Thelema is a philosophical and religious system. The central tenet of Thelema is "Do what thou wilt shall be the whole of the Law." This principle is based on the belief that each individual has the right to pursue their own true will without harmful interference from others. According to this belief, each individual has the right to live their life by their own true will. Thelema is also the name of Crowley's magical order, which he founded in 1907.

Thelemic Magick is a system of magickal practices based on Thelemic principles. Thelemic Magick emphasizes personal autonomy and freedom, and practitioners believe that each individual has the power to create their reality. It is designed to help the practitioner achieve their true will. Thelemic Magick is often seen as a more spiritual form of magic, as it is not focused on the material world. It also includes a belief in the power of symbols and rituals, and practitioners often use magickal rituals to manifest their desires.

The Connection between Maat Magick and Thelema

Maat Magick is based on the writings of Aleister Crowley, who was also the founder of the Thelemic system of magic. Maat Magick is an occult tradition that stresses the importance of balance and harmony in all things. Thelema, on the other hand, is a relatively new religious movement. At first glance, it may not seem like there would be much overlap between these two traditions. However, upon closer inspection, it becomes clear that there are several key similarities between Maat Magick and Thelema.

Both philosophies emphasize the importance of balance and self-control, and both encourage their followers to pursue their unique paths in life. In addition, both traditions place a great deal of emphasis on ritual and symbolism. As a result, it is not surprising that many people who practice Maat Magick also have an interest in Thelema. While Thelema may be a relatively new movement, it is clear that it has roots in some ancient ideas.

Both Maat Magick and Thelemic Magick emphasize personal autonomy and the power of the individual to create their reality. In addition, both systems believe in using symbols and rituals to manifest one's desires. The two traditions also share a belief in the importance of balance and harmony. As a result, it is not surprising that many people who practice Maat Magick also have an interest in Thelema.

However, there are also some key differences between Maat Magick and Thelemic Magick. One of the most notable differences is that Maat

Magick is focused on achieving balance in all areas of life. In contrast, Thelemic Magick primarily focuses on achieving the practitioner's true will. Another key difference is that Maat Magick is based on the energies of the Egyptian goddess Maat. In contrast, Thelemic Magick is based on the energies of the Greek god Pan.

Key Concepts in Maat Magick

Several key concepts are central to Maat Magick. It is a system of magic based on the principles of truth, balance, and justice. The goal of Maat Magick is to promote harmony and order in the world. Central to Maat Magick is the concept of Maat, the ancient Egyptian goddess of truth, justice, and balance.

To practice it, one must strive to uphold the values of truth, balance, and justice in all aspects of their life. This can be achieved by studying Maat's magical teachings, performing rituals and spells that align with her principles, and working to make the world more orderly and harmonious. By following the path of Maat Magick, practitioners can help create a more just and balanced world.

Here are some key concepts that are central to Maat Magick:

1. Liber Pennae Praenumbra

Liber Pennae Praenumbra, also known as the Book of Shadows, is a magical text used for centuries by witches. The book contains a variety of spells and rituals, as well as information on herbal lore and astrology. While the book's origins are unknown, it is believed to date back to the Middle Ages. Today, many modern witches use the Book of Shadows as a way to connect with their heritage.

For many Pagans, the book is seen as a sacred text that should be treated with respect. In recent years, there has been a resurgence of interest in the Book of Shadows, with new editions and versions being published regularly. Whether you are just beginning your exploration of witchcraft or you are a seasoned practitioner, the Book of Shadows is an essential part of the craft.

In Maat Magick, the Book of Shadows is used as a tool for self-discovery and personal growth. It is a way to connect with your higher self and the divine forces that guide your life. The book can be used as a journal, a grimoire, or simply as a place to collect your thoughts and musings.

The text of the Book of Shadows is not set in stone. Each witch should feel free to add or remove the content as they see fit. The only rule is that the book should be used for positive purposes. Anything harmful should be left out. With that in mind, here are some ideas to get you started:

- Use the Book of Shadows as a journal. Write down your thoughts and experiences with magic. This is a great way to track your progress and growth as a witch.
- Fill the book with spells and rituals that you find meaningful. This could include love spells, protection spells, or even simple rituals for self-care.
- Use the Book of Shadows as a grimoire. This is a place to record all the magical knowledge you have acquired. You can include information on herbs, crystals, and other tools of the trade.
- Use the book as a tool for divination. This could involve scrying, tarot readings, or any other form of divination to which you are drawn.
- Use the book as a tool for self-reflection. This is a place to explore your deepest thoughts and feelings. You can use it as a way to connect with your higher self and tap into your innate power.

2. Aeons

The concept of the Aeon is a central tenet of Maat Magick. An Aeon is a unit of time equal to 1,000 years. The current Aeon is that of Horus, which began in 2004 CE. The previous Aeon was that of Isis, and before that was the Aeon of Osiris. Each Aeon represents a different stage in humanity's spiritual evolution and is ruled by a particular deity. The Aeons are divided into stages known as sub-Aeons.

The current sub-Aeon is the Age of Horus, which began in 2004 CE and will last until the year 3000 CE. This was followed by the Age of Maat, which lasted from 3000 CE until 4000 CE. After that is the Age of Set, which will last from 4000 CE until 5000 CE. Finally, the Age of Nephthys will begin in 5000 CE and will last until 6000 CE.

Each sub-Aeon represents a different challenge that humanity must overcome on its journey to spiritual enlightenment. The Maat Magicians strive to align their own will with the divine will of the current Age to help usher in a new age of peace and harmony for all humanity.

3. Kabbalah

The Kabbalah is an ancient Jewish mysticism system that explores God's nature and the universe. It includes beliefs about the Creation, angels, and demons. The Kabbalah also teaches that everything in the universe is interconnected. This means that our actions can affect not only ourselves but also others and the world around us.

Maat Magick is a form of magic that incorporates these concepts. It seeks to bring about balance and order in the world. Maat Magick practitioners work to align themselves with the goddess Maat and her principles. This can be done through practices such as meditation, journaling, and working with magical tools such as crystals and tarot cards. By doing so, they hope to create a more just and harmonious world.

Maat and Kaballah are two systems of thought and practice that can be used together to create positive change in the world. When used together, they can help you connect with your higher self, the divine forces that guide your life, and the magic in the universe. The key is to remember that your thoughts and actions matter. What you do today can shape the world of tomorrow. So, let us all work together to create a more balanced and harmonious world.

4. The Tree of Life

The Tree of Life is a central concept in Maat Magick, which is based on ancient Egyptian cosmology. The tree is represented as a large tree with 10 branches, each representing a different aspect of reality. At the top of the tree is the Sun, representing the Divine light that illuminates all things. Below the Sun is the Moon and Stars, representing the cyclical nature of reality.

The tree of life.

Ausis.sk, CC BY-SA 4.0 <https://creativecommons.org/licenses/by-sa/4.0>, via Wikimedia Commons: https://commons.wikimedia.org/wiki/File:Stolna_lampa_Tree_of_Life_-_1631988313.png

The branches of the tree represent the five elements, Earth, Air, Fire, Water, and Spirit. These elements are, in turn, related to the five senses, body parts, and stages of life. Each element is also associated with a different color, planet, and tarot card.

The Tree of Life is used as a tool for self-reflection and self-development. By meditating on the tree, you can gain insights into your life and what it means. You can also use the tree to connect with the divine forces that guide your life. The key is to remember that the tree is a symbol, and its meaning is what you make of it.

The Tree of Life is thus a powerful symbol of both the unity and diversity of all things. It is a reminder that we are all connected and that our actions can have a ripple effect on the world around us. So let us all strive to live in harmony with the Tree of Life and create a more balanced and harmonious world for all.

5. N'Aton

N'Aton is the name of the sun god in ancient Egyptian mythology. He is often depicted as a hawk-headed man or a hawk-headed lion. N'Aton is associated with the element of fire and the color red. He is also associated with the planet Mars. N'Aton represents the active, masculine principle in the universe.

N'Aton is the creator god who gave birth to the other gods and goddesses. He is also the god of the sun, light, and truth. N'Aton is a powerful force for good, and his energy can be harnessed for positive change. When you work with N'Aton, you can tap into his power to create positive change in your life and the world around you.

N'Aton is a god of action, and his energy can be helpful when you need to take decisive action in your life. If you're facing a difficult situation, call on N'Aton for help. His energy can give you the strength and courage you need to overcome any obstacle.

According to Maat, N'Aton is the One True God, the source of all creation. By aligning ourselves with N'Aton, we can tap into that power and use it to create positive change in our lives. The key is to always act by Maat, the universal principle of truth and justice. When we do so, we are acting in harmony with the will of N'Aton. In doing so, we can bring about positive change in our lives and the world around us.

6. The Law of Return

The Law of Return is one of the basic principles of Maat Magick. It states that whatever energy you put into the universe will return to you threefold. In other words, if you do something positive, you'll receive three times the positive energy in return. Likewise, you'll receive three times the negative energy if you do something negative.

The Law of Return is a powerful tool for creating positive change in your life. By deliberately putting positive energy out into the world, you can attract more positivity into your life. This can help you manifest your desires and achieve your goals. Conversely, by avoiding negative actions and thoughts, you can reduce the amount of negativity in your life.

The Law of Return is a simple but powerful way to create positive change in your life. By aligning your actions with the positive principles of Maat, you can attract more positivity into your life and create the life you want.

7. Theurgy

One of the core concepts of Maat Magick is theurgy, which is the practice of using magical rituals to communicate with and invoke the gods. This contrasts with other forms of magic, which focus on manipulating energy or matter. Theurgy is based on the belief that the gods are real beings who can be contacted and influenced through ritual.

While the exact methods of communication vary from tradition to tradition, they typically involve some combination of prayer, offerings, and invocations. The goal of theurgy is to establish a relationship with the divine, to receive guidance, protection, or other favors. For many practitioners, theurgy is seen as a way to live in harmony with the natural order of things. By aligning oneself with the will of the gods, one can achieve a state of balance and harmony in one's own life.

8. Evocation

Evocation is the act of calling forth or summoning a deity and can be done for many reasons, such as to ask for guidance, to request healing, or simply to get in touch with the divine. There are many ways to evoke a spirit, but all require some level of focus and intention. The most important thing is to create an open and welcoming space. This can be done by setting up an altar with items representing the spirit you wish to call forth. It is also helpful to create a circle of protection, which will keep other energies from interfering with your work.

Once you have created this space, you can begin the evocation by calling out to the spirit by name. Be respectful and humble in your request, as evocation is a powerful act that should not be taken lightly. If done with pure intentions, evocation can be a very positive and transformative experience.

9. Invocation

When we talk about invocation in the context of Maat Magick, we are referring to the act of calling upon or summoning particular energy or entities into our lives. This can be done for various reasons, such as seeking guidance, protection, or healing. Invocation can be done either externally, by asking someone else to call on the energy on your behalf, or internally, through your practice. Regardless of how it is done, the goal is to create a space where you can connect with the energies you seek.

There are several ways to go about this, but your intention is key. When you are clear about what you hope to achieve through invocation, focusing your energies and calling upon the specific forces that can help you manifest your desires will be easier. In addition, it is important to create an atmosphere conducive to open communication and connection. This might involve smudging your space with sage or Palo Santo, lighting candles, or playing soothing music. Whatever you do, just ensure you set the stage for a positive and productive experience.

10. Sex Magick

In the world of magick, many different approaches can be taken to achieve specific goals. One approach that is sometimes used is sex magick. As the name suggests, sex magick involves using sexual energy to power magickal spells and rituals. While this may sound like a simple concept, a great deal of complexity is involved.

One of the key concepts in sex magick is the idea of consent. For sexual energy to be properly harnessed, all participants must be fully consenting and comfortable with the activity. This helps ensure that the resulting spell or ritual is performed with positive intentions and pure energy. Another important consideration in sex magick is the role of focus and visualization.

When performing a sex magick spell or ritual, it is crucial to focus on the desired outcome throughout the entire process. This can be facilitated by using specific visualization techniques, such as picturing the desired result while masturbating or creating a mental image of the desired outcome during intercourse. By keeping these concepts in mind, anyone can learn to harness the power of sex magick.

Maat Magick and Its Place in Today's World

Maat Magickers have practiced their craft in secret for centuries. Still, in recent years there has been a resurgence of interest in this type of magic. People are drawn to the idea of a spiritual practice rooted in tradition but still relevant to modern life. Maat Magick teaches that all things are interconnected and that we must strive for balance in all areas of our lives. This includes our relationships with the natural world, interactions with others, and even our thoughts and emotions. When we are out of balance, it can lead to disharmony and suffering. However, by aligning ourselves with Maat, we can bring positive change to our lives and the world around us.

There is a growing interest in shamanism, energy work, and other alternative spiritual practices in today's world. Maat Magick offers a unique path combining many elements into a cohesive system. It is a practice based on respect for the natural world, reverence for the divine, and a commitment to personal growth. As we continue to face challenges in our world, such as climate change, economic inequality, and social injustice, Maat Magick provides a framework for working towards positive solutions. If you are interested in exploring this type of magic, several resources are available to help you get started.

Maat Magick is a type of magic rooted in tradition but still relevant to modern life. It teaches that all things are interconnected and that we must strive for balance in all areas of our lives. This includes our relationships with the natural world, interactions with others, and even our thoughts and emotions. The key concepts discussed in this chapter are some of the reasons why Maat Magick is gaining popularity in today's world. Its focus on personal growth and social responsibility provides a much-needed alternative to mainstream spiritual practices.

Chapter 8: Magickal Ceremonies and Rituals

The ancient Egyptians believed that Maat was essential for maintaining balance in the universe. This concept of Maat was central to Egyptian cosmology and ethics. The Egyptians believed that upholding Maat was necessary for one's well-being and the stability of society and cosmic order. To uphold Maat, they used a variety of rituals and ceremonies, such as offering prayers and sacrifices to the gods, performing purification rites, and participating in processions and festivals. By upholding Maat's principles of truth, justice, and balance, they ensured their well-being and the health of their society and the cosmos.

Maat Magick is an ancient Egyptian system of magick that can be used to improve your life in several ways. This chapter will focus on the benefits of practicing Maat Magick and how to perform various Maat Magick rituals. You'll learn about protection, warding, banishing, consecration, and invocation rituals. By incorporating these rituals into your life, you can improve your focus, connect with the divine, develop your intuition, strengthen your willpower, and more.

Benefits of Practicing Maat Magick

Many people turn to magick to bring about positive change in their lives. While there are many different magick traditions, Maat Magick is one of the most rewarding. Here are some of the many benefits of practicing Maat Magick.

1. Helps Focus the Mind

One of the most important benefits of practicing Maat Magick is that it helps to focus the mind. It can be easy to become scattered and unfocused in our busy, modern lives. By contrast, the disciplined study of Maat Magick requires concentration and mental focus. As a result, those who practice this form of magic often find that their minds are better able to meet the challenges of everyday life. In addition, this practice can help develop greater self-awareness, which can lead to a greater sense of peace and well-being. For these reasons, anyone seeking to improve their mental focus and clarity would do well to consider practicing Maat Magick.

2. Connects You with the Divine

Maat Magick is a system of spiritual beliefs and practices that involves the invocation of the Egyptian goddess Maat. Followers of Maat believe that by aligning themselves with her principles, they can achieve personal transformation and connect with the divine. Maat Magick emphasizes ethics, morality, and living in balance with the natural world. Its practitioners believe that by adhering to Maat's code of conduct, they can achieve spiritual enlightenment and become closer to the gods.

The path of Maat is one of self-improvement and self-awakening, and its ultimate goal is to become closer to the divine. Her teachings can be applied to every aspect of life, from relationships to work to finances. Her followers believe that by living according to her principles, they will find harmony and fulfillment in all areas of their lives. Suppose you are searching for a spiritual path that emphasizes personal growth and connection with the divine. In that case, Maat Magick may be right for you.

3. Develops Your Intuition

One of the benefits of practicing Maat Magick is that it helps develop your intuition. Intuition is defined as the ability to understand something immediately without the need for conscious reasoning. When you practice Maat Magick, you connect with your subconscious mind, where your intuition resides. As you become more attuned to your intuition, you'll find that you can make decisions more quickly and efficiently. You'll also become better at "reading" people and situations and less likely to be caught off-guard by unexpected events.

Developing your intuition through Maat Magick can help you lead a more prosperous life. Many of the world's most successful people have relied on their intuition to guide them to success. If you would like to tap into this powerful source of knowledge, Maat Magick can help you do so. It can also help you develop other psychic abilities, such as clairvoyance and precognition.

4. Improves Your Creativity

When you engage in Maat Magick, you tap into your innate creativity. This type of magick allows you to explore different aspects of your personality and bring forth your hidden talents. The act of creating something from nothing is a powerful act of will, and it can have a profound effect on your life. By its very nature, Maat Magick encourages you to think outside the box and to come up with new and innovative solutions to problems.

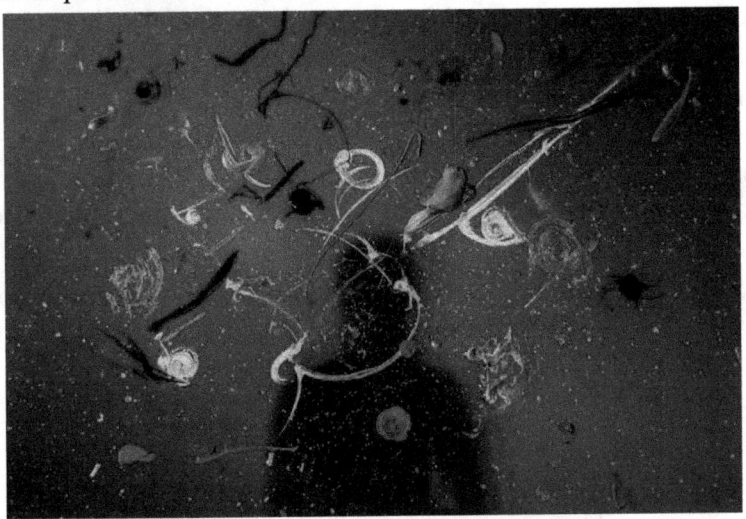

Maat Magic helps you connect with your creativity.
https://unsplash.com/photos/SPTh4rzR6xQ?utm_source=unsplash&utm_medium=referral&utm_content=creditShareLink

In addition, the process of creating magickal rituals and spells can help to hone your creative skills. As you become more adept at crafting magickal formulas, you'll find that your creativity will flourish in other areas of your life as well. Whether you are an artist, a writer, or simply someone who enjoys coming up with new ideas, practicing Maat Magick can help you unleash your full potential.

5. Strengthens Your Willpower

One of the benefits of practicing Maat Magick is that it strengthens your willpower. Willpower is the ability to resist temptation and stick to your goals. It is a critical ingredient in success. When you have strong willpower, you are more likely to achieve your goals. And when you practice Maat Magick, you constantly affirm your commitment to truth and justice. This strengthens your willpower and resolve.

In addition, the practice of Maat Magick helps you to develop self-discipline. This is because you are constantly working on mastering your thoughts, emotions, and actions. As you become more disciplined, your willpower will also increase. So, if you are looking for a way to boost your willpower, consider practicing Maat Magick.

It can help you to create positive change in your own life. Suppose you are struggling with addiction or negative patterns of behavior. In that case, Maat Magick can provide you with the tools you need to break free and start fresh. In addition, practicing it can help you develop a stronger connection with the natural world.

By attuning yourself to the cycles of nature, you can learn to live in greater harmony with the earth. Finally, Maat Magick can also be a source of strength and support during difficult times. When the world feels out of balance, practitioners of Maat Magick can draw on their power to help restore harmony.

Whether you are looking for personal transformation or ways to make a difference in the world, Maat Magick is a powerful tradition worth exploring.

Protection Rituals

Maat Magick practitioners seek to maintain balance through the use of protection rituals. These rituals can take many forms, but all are designed to ward off negative energy and forces. Common ingredients in protection spells include salt, herbs, and protective amulets. Maat Magicians may also use gestures and words of power to create an invisible barrier of protection around themselves or their homes. Here are some examples of protection rituals that you can try:

1. The Mooncup Rite

The Mooncup Rite is a simple but powerful protection ritual that can be performed at any time, provided you have a lunar phase cup or chalice. This cup is filled with sacred water from a natural source, such as a lake, river, spring, or well. Once the moonlight has been drawn into the water, it is then used to cleanse your body and aura. The entire process takes less than an hour and can be done alone or with others. Maat Magick Protection Ritual offers a simple way to cleanse and protect yourself from negativity.

2. The Mass of Maat

This protection ritual is a simple but powerful way to shield yourself from negative energy. The ritual involves invoking the Egyptian goddess Maat, who is the personification of truth, justice, and balance. Once you have invoked Maat, you visualize her holding a scale in her hands. On one side of the scale is your heart, and on the other is a feather. If your heart is heavier than a feather, then it means that you are out of balance and carrying too much negative energy. Maat will then help cleanse and purify your heart, returning you to a state of balance. This ritual can be performed as often as needed and is an excellent way to protect yourself from negative influences.

3. The Rite of the Children

In this rite, which is also known as the Rite of the Children, participants invoke Maat's power to shield themselves from harm. The ritual begins with the drawing of a circle on the ground. Inside the circle, a small child is seated on a stool or chair. The child is then wrapped in a blanket or cloak representing Maat's protective wings. Next, the other participants stand around the circle and chant an invocation to Maat. Once the ritual is complete, everyone feels a sense of peace and calm, knowing that they are safe from harm.

4. The Dance of the Mask

The Dance of the Mask is a powerful ritual that can help you cleanse your aura and release any unwanted energy. To perform this ritual, you'll need a white mask and a black scarf. Begin by donning the mask and tying the scarf around your head so that it covers your eyes. Take a few deep breaths and visualize yourself surrounded by white light. As you breathe in, imagine the light entering your body and cleansing your aura. Then, begin to dance around the room, moving your body in whatever way feels natural. Continue dancing until you feel like all of the negative energy has been released. Once you are finished, sit down and thank the Universe for providing you with this protection.

Warding Rituals

One of the most important aspects of Maat Magick is warding. A ward is a protective barrier that can be used to keep out negative energy and entities. There are many different types of wards, and each practitioner develops their own unique methods. However, some common elements are often used in Maat Magick warding rituals.

One of the most important ingredients is salt. Salt is known for its ability to absorb negative energy, and it is often used in cleansing and protection rituals. It can be used to create a circle of protection around an area, or it can be sprinkled on objects that you wish to protect.

Herbs are also commonly used in warding rituals. Popular choices include lavender (for peace and relaxation), rosemary (for purification), and basil (for strength and courage). These herbs can be burned as incense, carried in sachets, or scattered around an area that you wish to protect. Using these simple ingredients, you can create strong wards that will help keep negative energy at bay.

1. The Eye of Horus

The Eye of Horus is an ancient Egyptian symbol of protection, royal power, and good health. The Eye of Horus was often used as a protective amulet and was often painted on the inside of coffins and tombs. The Eye of Horus is also known as the wedjat, wadjat, or udjat eye. The Eye of Horus is representative of the god Horus as the protector and avenger of Egypt. The Eye of Horus is a very powerful symbol, and many people still use it today as a protective charm.

There are several ways to perform the Eye of Horus warding ritual. One way is to take an egg and draw the Eye of Horus on it with a black magic marker. Place the egg in a safe place where it will not be disturbed. Another way to perform the ritual is to write the name "Horus" on a piece of paper and place it under your pillow while you sleep. This will help to protect you from harm while you sleep. Finally, you can also wear an amulet or talisman that has the Eye of Horus symbol on it. This will help to protect you from negative energy and keep you safe from harm.

2. The Feather of Maat

The Feather of Maat is an ancient Egyptian warding ritual still used by modern-day practitioners. The ritual involves placing a feather on the doorstep of a home or business, which is said to ward off negative energy and forces. The Feather of Maat is named after the Egyptian goddess of truth and justice, who was often depicted with a feather in her hair. In addition to being used as a protective charm, the Feather of Maat ritual can also be used to bring justice and balance to the world. Those who perform the ritual believe that by doing so, they are helping to bring about Maat's vision for a just and harmonious world.

3. The Ankh of Isis

The Ankh of Isis is a Maat Magick warding ritual used to protect against negative energies. The ritual involves drawing an Ankh on the ground with a piece of chalk, then walking around the perimeter of the Ankh three times while chanting a protective mantra. The mantra can be anything from a simple prayer to a more complex magical incantation. The important thing is that it is recited with intention and focus. Once the ritual is complete, the Ankh should be left in place for as long as possible to provide maximum protection. This simple but powerful ritual can be performed by anyone, regardless of their level of magical knowledge or experience.

4. The Djed Pillar

The Djed Pillar is a popular ritual used in Maat Magick to protect against negative energies. The ritual involves drawing a symbolic pillar on the ground and using salt and water to create a barrier around the pillar. Once the pillar is complete, you then recite a powerful incantation that calls on the forces of good to protect you from harm. This ritual can be customized to fit your specific needs and is often used in combination with other Maat Magick rituals. Whether you are looking to ward off evil spirits or simply create a sense of protection, the Djed Pillar can be a powerful tool in your magickal arsenal.

Banishing Rituals

If you are looking for a way to banish negative energy and cleanse your space, consider trying a Maat Magick banishing ritual. There are several different ways to perform a banishing ritual. Here are a few of the most popular:

1. The Cleansing Flame

If you're looking to banish negativity from your life, the Cleansing Flame ritual is a great way to start. This simple but effective ritual uses the element of fire to cleanse away all unwanted energies. The first step is to write down all of the negativity that you want to banish on a piece of paper. This could be anything from envy and jealousy to anger and hatred. Once you have a complete list, it's time to light it on fire. You can do this using a candle, lighter, or even a match. As the paper burns, visualize all the negative energy released from your life. Allow the paper to burn completely, and then dispose of the ashes in a safe place.

2. The Burning Bowl

The Burning Bowl is a banishing ritual that is designed to remove negative energy from your life. To begin, you'll need a candle and a fireproof bowl or cauldron. Place the bowl in the center of your workspace and light the candle. Focus your intention on the flame and visualize all of your negativity being drawn into the flame. As you do this, say aloud or in your mind: "I banish all negativity from my life. I release all fear, anger, and pain. I am surrounded by light and love." Allow the candle to burn for as long as you feel it is necessary, then blow it out. Thank the element of fire for its help, and know that you have taken an important step towards banishing negativity from your life.

3. The Banishment of Set

Set is an ancient Egyptian god associated with chaos, disorder, and violence. In many ways, he personifies the very worst aspects of human nature. For this reason, some practitioners of Maat Magick perform a ritual banishing Set when they wish to rid themselves of negative influences.

The ritual is relatively simple. First, the practitioner summons Set forth into the world using a statement of intent. Then they visualize Set being banished from their presence, driven away by the light of Maat. Finally, they release Set back into the chaotic void from which he came.

Though it may seem like a small thing, this ritual can be quite powerful. By banishing Set, we cast out the destructive forces that can hinder our growth and development. In doing so, we create space for positive change and transformation in our lives.

Consecration Rituals

Consecration rituals are an important part of Maat Magick. They are used to cleanse and purify objects that will be used in spells or rituals. Consecration can also be used to consecrate a space, such as an altar or circle. There are many different ways to perform a consecration ritual, but they all share certain basic elements. First, the object or space to be consecrated is cleansed with water. This represents the element of water and the purity of Maat. Next, salt is added to the water. This represents the element of earth and grounding energy. Finally, the mixture is blessed with the words, "I purify and consecrate this (object or space) in the name of Maat." This completes the ritual and infuses the object or space with positive, magical energy.

Invocation Rituals

Maat Magick is an ancient Egyptian system of magic and spirituality that can be used to achieve a variety of different goals. One of the most popular applications of Maat Magick is invocation, which is the act of calling upon a higher power to help achieve a specific goal. There are many different ways to perform an invocation, but all of them involve some form of ritualistic behavior. For example, some people may light candles or burn incense as part of their invocation, while others may recite specific prayers or chants. No matter what form it takes, an invocation is a powerful tool that can help you achieve your goals.

Maat Magick is a system of magic and spirituality that can be used to achieve a variety of different goals. It is based on the ancient Egyptian goddess Maat, who represents truth, justice, and balance. This chapter has discussed some of the most important aspects of Maat Magick, including the elements, principles, and rituals. Consecration rituals are used to cleanse and purify objects that will be used in spells or rituals. Invocation rituals are used to call on a higher power to help achieve a specific goal.

Chapter 9: Prayers and Meditations

The ancient Egyptians were deeply spiritual people, and prayer was an integral part of their lives. Prayer was a way to connect with the gods and goddesses and ask for their help or guidance. There are many different types of Kemetic prayers, from short invocations to long and detailed hymns. In this chapter, we will explore some of the most common prayers and meditations used by the ancient Egyptians.

Coming Up with Your Prayers

Remember that the gods and goddesses are always listening when creating your prayers. You can pray to them for anything, big or small. It is also important to be as specific as possible when asking for help or guidance. The more specific you are, the easier it will be for the gods to understand your needs. Here are some tips to help you get started:

1. Start by deciding who you want to pray to. This can be any of the Egyptian gods or goddesses. You can even pray to multiple deities at once.
2. Think about what you want to ask for. Be as specific as possible.
3. Choose the type of prayer that you feel best suits your needs.
4. Find a quiet place where you can focus and relax.
5. Take a few deep breaths and allow yourself to become calm and centered.

6. Begin your prayer. You can either speak aloud or silently in your mind.
7. Once you are finished, take a moment to thank the gods for their time and assistance.
8. You can now carry on with your day, knowing that the gods are with you.

Prayer to Ra
"O Ra, lord of the sun,
I pray to you for strength and courage.
I ask that you shine your light upon my heart,
And guide me through the darkness."

Prayer to Bast
"O Bast, goddess of cats and protector of the home,
I pray to you for protection.
I ask that you watch over me and my family,
And keep us safe from harm."

Prayer to Ptah
"O Ptah, god of art and creation,
I pray to you for inspiration.
I ask that you spark creativity in my heart,
And help me to see the beauty in all things."

Prayer to Sobek
"O Sobek, god of the Nile and protector of crocodiles,
I pray to you for strength and power.
I ask that you give me the courage to face my fears,
And the strength to overcome them."

Prayer to Hathor
"O Hathor, goddess of love and beauty,
I pray to you for happiness.
I ask that you fill my heart with love,
And help me to find joy in all things."

Prayer to Osiris
"O Osiris, god of the underworld and judge of the dead,

I pray to you for guidance.
I ask that you help me to find my way,
And show me the path to righteousness."

Prayer to Isis
"O Isis, goddess of motherhood and healing,
I pray to you for comfort.
I ask that you ease my pain and suffering,
And help me to find peace."

Prayer to Horus
"O Horus, god of the sky and protector of the Pharaoh,
I pray to you for victory.
I ask that you give me the strength to fight,
And the power to triumph."

Prayer to Maat
"O Maat, goddess of truth and justice,
I pray to you for balance.
I ask that you help me to see both sides of every issue,
And to find the middle path."

Maat Meditations

The Nile Meditation

The Nile Meditation is a Maat Meditation that can be used to connect with the energies of the Nile River. The Nile is one of the most powerful rivers in the world and has been a source of life for countless generations. By connecting with the energies of the Nile, you can access a deep well of wisdom and strength.

The meditation begins by imagining yourself standing at the edge of the Nile. You see your reflection staring back at you as you look out over the water. Take a moment to focus on your reflection and connect with your inner wisdom. Then, begin to imagine the flow of the river around you. Feel the cool water flowing past your feet and the warm sun on your skin. As you breathe in, feel yourself drawing in the power of the river.

Allow yourself to be filled with the strength of the Nile. Hold this energy within you for a few moments before releasing it back into the flow of the river. As you release the energy, feel your connection to the river deepening. Allow yourself to be filled with a sense of peace and well-being. When you are ready, bring your awareness back to your surroundings and take a few deep breaths before carrying on with your day.

The Eye of Ra Meditation

The Eye of Ra Meditation is a Maat Meditation that can be used to connect with the energies of the sun god, Ra. He is the lord of the sun and one of the most powerful gods in the Egyptian pantheon. By connecting with his energy, you can access a deep well of strength and courage.

The meditation begins by imagining yourself standing in the presence of Ra. Feel the warmth of the sun on your skin and the power of Ra's energy radiating around you. As you breathe in, draw in the energy of the sun god. Allow yourself to be filled with his strength.

Then, begin to imagine the sun itself. Feel the warmth of its rays on your skin and the power of its light shining down on you. As you breathe in, draw in the energy of the sun. Allow yourself to be filled with its power. Finally, begin to imagine yourself as the sun. Feel the power of your light shining down on the world.

The Feather of Maat Meditation

The Feather of Maat Meditation is a Maat Meditation that can be used to connect with the energies of truth and justice. Maat is the goddess of truth and justice, and her feather is a symbol of balance. Connecting with her energy allows you to access a deep well of wisdom and strength.

The meditation begins by imagining yourself standing in the presence of Maat. As you look at her, you see her holding a feather in her hand. Take a moment to focus on the feather and feel its energy radiating around you. As you breathe in, draw in the energy of the feather. Allow yourself to be filled with Maat's truth and justice.

Then, begin to imagine the feather itself. Feel the lightness of its touch and the power of its presence. As you breathe in, draw in the energy of the feather. Allow yourself to be filled with its power. As you move through the world, feel yourself spreading the energies of truth and justice.

Meditation and prayers are powerful tools that can help you connect with the energies of the Egyptian gods and goddesses. This chapter has provided you with different meditations and prayers that you can use to connect with the energies of the Egyptian gods and goddesses. By connecting with these energies, you can access a deep well of wisdom and strength. Choose a meditation or prayer that resonates with you and use it as a tool to help you through your journey.

Chapter 10: Adding Maat into Modern Life

The Egyptian goddess Maat was the personification of truth, justice, balance, and order. The ancient Egyptians believed that if they followed the 42 precepts of Maat, they would lead a righteous life that would be pleasing to the gods and result in success and happiness in this world and the next. Although we do not live in ancient Egypt, we can still learn from and apply the wisdom of Maat to our modern lives.

This chapter will explore some of how we can do this. We will first look at some of the main rules of Maat and what they mean. We will then explore various ways in which we can incorporate these principles into our modern lives.

Following the Rules of Maat

The 42 precepts of Maat were compiled by the ancient Egyptians. They cover a wide range of topics, from respect for the gods and one's parents to justice, truthfulness, moderation, and more. These 42 rules were discussed in Chapter 3, but there are various actions we can take in life to help us follow them.

Respecting the Gods

The ancient Egyptians believed that the gods were responsible for everything in the world, from the weather to human prosperity. They believed that it was crucial to show respect for the gods to maintain their favor. There are various ways in which we can do this in our modern lives. We can learn about ancient Egypt's different gods and goddesses and what they represented. This means believing in them and honoring them with our words and deeds.

In modern times, we might not have traditional gods that we worship, but we can still respect and honor whatever it is that we believe in. Whether it is the Christian god, Allah, Buddha, or something else entirely, we can show our respect by living our lives by their teachings.

Honoring Your Parents

Respect for one's parents was another significant value in ancient Egyptian society. The Egyptians believed that it was crucial to honor one's parents to maintain their favor and support. In our modern lives, we can still honor our parents by showing them respect, listening to their advice, and following their example. We can also show them appreciation by doing things for them, such as cooking their favorite meal, taking them on a special outing, or just spending time with them.

Making Amends

If someone broke any of the rules of Maat, they were required to make amends. This could involve anything from apologizing to the person they had harmed to making a sacrifice to the gods. In our modern lives, we can still make amends when we have done something wrong. We can apologize to the person we have harmed and try to make things right. We can also learn from our mistakes and try to do better in the future. This is an essential part of living a life by the principles of Maat.

Speaking the Truth

In many cultures, speaking the truth is seen as a virtue, and those who lie or spread falsehoods are often looked down upon. In some cases, such as in courtrooms or during business deals, telling the truth is legally required. However, even in everyday life, speaking honestly is generally considered to be the best policy. When we are truthful with others, we build trust and create relationships based on mutual respect.

Truthfulness was an important value in ancient Egyptian society. In our modern lives, we can still strive to be truthful in our words and actions. We can also help others to speak the truth by being open and honest with them. So next time you're tempted to say something that isn't true, think of Maat and let your conscience guide you.

Acting with Justice

One way that individuals could uphold Maat was by being just in their daily lives. This meant not only treating others fairly but also taking responsibility for one's actions. In our modern lives, we can still strive to act with justice. We can treat others fairly, regardless of their race, religion, or any other characteristic. We can also work to hold ourselves and others accountable for our actions. This includes taking responsibility for our own choices and being willing to face the consequences of our actions.

Respecting Life

One of the most important tenants of Maat is respect for life. This includes both human and animal life. The Egyptians believed that all life was sacred and should be treated with care and compassion. To harm another creature was to invite chaos and disorder into one's own life. By following the principle of respect for life, we can help create a more peaceful and harmonious world. When we show kindness and respect to those around us, we create positive energy that can flow out into the universe.

Caring for the Environment

Showing respect to the environment is a way to uphold Maat.
https://unsplash.com/photos/SPTh4rzR6xQ?utm_source=unsplash&utm_medium=referral&utm_content=creditShareLink

Another way to uphold Maat is by respecting the environment. In ancient times, the Egyptians believed that the gods resided in nature and often built temples and shrines in natural settings. They also depended on the Nile River for their livelihood, and they took care to avoid harming the plants and animals that lived there. In our modern lives, we can still show respect for the environment. We can do that by not polluting. We can also work to protect endangered species and their habitats.

Being Generous

One way to follow the Rule of Maat was to be generous. Generosity was seen as a way of restoring balance and harmony. It was believed that giving generously of one's time, talents, and resources could help bring about a more just and peaceful world. In today's world, the idea of being generous may seem like a simple act of kindness. However, it is still an important value to uphold. By being generous, we can help make the world a better place for everyone.

Staying Pure

The ancient Egyptians believed in the principle of Maat, which can be roughly translated as balance or order. To them, Maat was the ideal state of both the individual and the universe, and they strove to live by its teachings. One of the key aspects of Maat was purity, both in terms of physical cleanliness and morals. The Egyptians believed that by maintaining their purity, they could keep the world in balance.

In practical terms, this meant that they would bathe regularly and avoid eating unclean foods. They would dress modestly and abstain from activities that might be considered morally questionable. By following the rule of Maat, the Egyptians hoped to achieve a state of harmony both within themselves and in the world around them.

Observing Moderation

This rule of Maat is an ancient Egyptian principle that promotes balance and moderation in all things. The goddess Maat personifies this ideal, and her name is often used to refer to the concept of truth, justice, and order. In practical terms, the rule of Maat means living in harmony with oneself and one's environment. It is about finding the middle way between extremes and avoiding excessive behaviors. This can apply to everything from diet and exercise to work and relationships. By following the rule of

Maat, we can create a more balanced and sustainable way of life.

Following the Righteous Path

In ancient Egypt, Pharaohs were considered to be mediators between the gods and humans, and they were responsible for maintaining Maat. To achieve this, they had to follow the path of righteousness. If they strayed from Maat, they would be judged by Osiris, the god of the dead. The judgment would be based on their deeds during their lifetime. If they were found wanting, they would be cast into the underworld.

Therefore, following the path of righteousness was essential for avoiding eternal damnation. Today, we can still learn from the ancient Egyptians by following the principles of Maat in our own lives. By living truthfully, justly, and harmoniously, we can create a more balanced and ordered world for ourselves and future generations.

Subordinating Your Desires

This rule of Maat is an ancient Egyptian principle that can be traced back to the time of the Pharaohs. The word Maat refers to truth, justice, and balance, and the principle of Maat dictates that one should live their life in a way that upholds these values. In practice, this means subordinating your desires in favor of what is right and good.

It is easy to become caught up in our wants and needs, but if we take a step back and consider the effect our actions will have on others, it becomes clear that sometimes it is necessary to put aside our interests for the greater good. When doing so, we help create a more just and harmonious world for all.

Resisting Temptation

In ancient Egyptian society, it was believed that upholding Maat's principles would bring one prosperity and good fortune. Central to this is the idea of resisting temptation. In a world where it is so easy to give in to our desires, self-control can seem like a difficult task. However, the rewards of following Maat's teachings are worth the effort. When we resist temptation, we build character and strength of will. We also learn to be content with what we have instead of constantly chasing after what we want.

Making Sacrifices

In Egyptian society, it was believed that balance was essential for both individual and communal harmony. As such, many people made sacrifices to the goddess. These could be material offerings, such as food or jewelry, or they could be more abstract, such as acts of self-denial or giving up bad habits. By making sacrifices to Maat, people hoped to achieve balance in their own lives and make a positive contribution to the world around them. While material possessions can be valuable, they are not the only things worth sacrificing for. Sometimes, it is more important to sacrifice our time, energy, or even our happiness for the sake of others.

Giving Thanks

Giving thanks is an important part of following the Rule of Maat. Her name means "the right way" or "the truth." The Rule of Maat is based on the principles of truth, justice, balance, and order. It is the belief that these principles should guide our lives.

When we give thanks, we acknowledge that we have received something of value. We are also indicating our willingness to reciprocate in some way. By giving thanks, we show our respect for things' natural order. We are also demonstrating our commitment to following the Rule of Maat.

Seeking Forgiveness

Many people seek forgiveness without really understanding what it is they are asking for. They may approach forgiveness as though it is a simple transaction. For example, they did something wrong, and now they want to be forgiven so that they can move on with their lives. However, forgiveness is not that simple. True forgiveness requires both parties to understand what happened and to come to a place of resolution. Without this understanding, the hurt and anger can continue to fester, leading to resentment and bitterness.

The Egyptian concept of Maat provides a helpful framework for understanding how to seek forgiveness in a way that can lead to healing and reconciliation. Maat is based on the idea of truth and balance. When someone has harmed another, they must take responsibility for their actions and make things right. This may involve apologizing, making restitution, or even suffering consequences. Only then can true forgiveness occur. By taking the time to seek forgiveness in a way that promotes healing and reconciliation, we can create relationships that are based on respect and trust.

Repenting Your Mistakes

According to the ancient Egyptian teachings of Maat, each person is responsible for their actions and must seek to balance themselves spiritually. One way to achieve this balance is by repenting of your mistakes. To do this, you must first take responsibility for your actions and then take steps to make amends. This may involve apologizing to those you have harmed, or it could mean donating to a worthy cause. By taking these steps, you can help to restore balance in your life and become a better person. Ultimately, following the teachings of Maat can lead to a more fulfilling and peaceful life.

Understanding the Afterlife

The ancient Egyptians believed in an afterlife and had elaborate rituals and beliefs surrounding death. According to this belief, the soul had to be in balance for it to achieve immortality. The weighing of the heart was a ritual that was performed after death, and it determined whether the soul was pure enough to enter the afterlife. If the heart was heavier than a feather, it meant that the soul was unbalanced and would be devoured by a monster. However, if the heart was lighter than a feather, it meant that the soul was in harmony and would be allowed to enter the afterlife. The rule of Maat was just one of many beliefs that the ancient Egyptians had about death and the afterlife.

Persevering through Adversity

The ancient Egyptians believed that life was a journey and that we all had to persevere through difficult times. They believed that by enduring difficult challenges, we could become better people. This is a core principle of the Rule of Maat. By facing adversity and overcoming it, we can learn and grow. We can also become more compassionate and understanding towards others. When we persevere through tough times, we are not only making ourselves stronger but also helping to create a better world.

Trusting the Gods

According to the ancient Egyptian belief system, the gods were responsible for maintaining balance in the universe. The idea of trusting in the gods to maintain balance might seem strange to us today, but it was an essential part of Ancient Egyptian beliefs. The Egyptians believed that everything in the universe was connected and that humans were just a small part of a much larger whole.

As such, they saw it as their responsibility to uphold the Maat and keep things in harmony. This could be done through individual actions, such as leading a good life, or through communal efforts, such as working together to build temples and pyramids. By following the Rule of Maat, Ancient Egyptians hoped to maintain balance in their lives and the universe.

Being Kind

Being kind is one of the most important things we can do. It doesn't cost anything and can make a difference in someone's life. Every day, we have opportunities to be kind to others. We can smile at someone, offer a compliment, or perform a random act of kindness. When we take the time to be kind, we spread positive energy and goodwill. And that's always a good thing.

There are also many benefits to being kind. Studies have shown that kindness is associated with lower levels of stress hormones, blood pressure, anxiety, and depression. It can also improve our immune system and provide us with a sense of satisfaction and well-being. So next time you have an opportunity to be kind, go for it.

Helping the Needy

For centuries, cultures around the world have held to the belief that those who have been blessed with good fortune should share their blessings with those less fortunate. This idea is summed up in the Egyptian concept of Maat, which calls for individuals to behave in ways that promote balance and harmony. One way to uphold Maat is by helping those in need.

Whether it is lending a hand to a neighbor or volunteering at a local soup kitchen, acts of kindness can help to create a sense of community and bring people together. In a world that is often filled with conflict and division, following the Rule of Maat can be a powerful way to bring about positive change.

Leading a Modest Life

This rule of Maat is the ancient Egyptian philosophy that calls for balance, moderation, and truth in all things. It is based on the idea that the world is a constantly changing and chaotic place and that by living a modest life, we can maintain order and harmony. This philosophy can be applied to many areas of our lives but is especially relevant when it comes to material possessions.

In a world where we are constantly bombarded with advertising and messages telling us to buy more stuff, it can be difficult to resist the temptation to accumulate material possessions. However, if we remember the rule of Maat, we can lead more modest lives and focus on what is truly important. When we live in moderation, we create space in our lives for experiences and relationships that are more important than material things.

We become less bound by our possessions and freer to pursue our dreams and goals. So next time you are feeling the urge to splurge on something new, take a moment to reflect on the rule of Maat. By leading a life of moderation, you can create a richer, more fulfilling life for yourself and those around you.

Being Patient

In our lives, we can think of patience as our feather. We can use it to weigh our hearts and see if we are living in a state of balance. Just as Maat represents truth and justice, patience represents balance. When we are patient, we are able to see both sides of a situation and make decisions based on what is fair and just. We are also able to let go of our egos and accept things as they are. As a result, patience is often seen as a virtue, a quality that can help us lead more balanced and fulfilling lives.

Tips for Upholding Maat in Everyday Life

Fortunately, you don't need to be a goddess to live a life by Maat. You can do many simple things to make sure you are living ethically and in harmony with the world around you. Here are a few additional tips:

- Be honest in your interactions with others. This doesn't mean you have to share everything about yourself, but it does mean being truthful when asked direct questions.

- Respect the property of others. This includes physical belongings and things like ideas and creative works. Give credit where it's due, and don't take things that don't belong to you.
- Be considerate of others' feelings. This includes both speaking and listening respectfully. Avoid saying or doing hurtful things, even if you're joking. If someone has wronged you, try to see their side of the story before getting angry.
- Be environmentally responsible. Take care of the planet we all share by recycling, reducing waste, and conserving energy and resources.

Of course, this is just a small sampling of ways to live according to Maat. The most important thing is to be conscious of your actions and their impact on yourself and those around you. Living with integrity and respect can help create a more harmonious world for all.

The rule of Maat is a powerful philosophy that can help us to lead more balanced and fulfilling lives. By being honest, respectful, and considerate of others, we can create a more harmonious world for all. And by being patient and living in moderation, we can free up time and space in our lives for truly important things. So next time you're feeling lost in the material world, remember the rules of Maat and strive to live a life of balance and harmony.

Conclusion

When we live our lives by the teachings of Maat, we create balance and harmony both within ourselves and in the world around us. We become more attuned to the natural rhythms of life and the Universe, and we are better able to weather the ups and downs that inevitably come our way. By living according to Maat, we not only honor the Goddess and the ancient Kemetic traditions, but we also set ourselves on the path to a more fulfilling and joyful life.

This comprehensive guide has hopefully given you a good introduction to the Kemetic religion and the goddess Maat. Many resources are available online and in print if you want to learn more. The best way to learn is to find a local community or group you can connect with in person. There is nothing quite like learning from and sharing experiences with others who are on the same spiritual path as you.

In this easy-to-understand book, we have covered the history and origins of Maat. We have also discussed the 7 principles and 42 laws that form the foundation of this ancient Egyptian religion. You have learned about some of the most important deities in Kemeticism and how to honor them in your own life. We have talked about the importance of ancestors and how to build a shrine to honor them. Finally, we have explored how you can incorporate Maat into your modern life through magick, meditation, and prayer.

While there is much to learn about Maat and Kemeticism, this book has hopefully given you a good foundation on which to build. Using the information and resources in this book, you can begin to create your relationship with Maat and start living a more balanced and harmonious life. Take your time, go at your own pace, and listen to your heart. Through our journey of self-discovery, we truly understand the goddess Maat and all that she represents.

Part 2: Ancient Egyptian Magic

The Ultimate Guide to Gods, Goddesses, Divination, Amulets, Rituals, and Spells of Ancient Egypt

Introduction

Have you ever wondered about the ancient Egyptian religion? Perhaps you have wondered what deities they worshiped and what sort of magic they practiced.

Even though ancient Egyptian religion and magic may seem like relics of a bygone era, they have fascinated people for generations and still do to this day. Numerous hermetic orders have incorporated Egyptian magic and religion into their practices. Orders such as the Rosicrucian Order, Hermetic Order of the Golden Dawn, and Stella Matutina incorporated many Egyptian beliefs into their practices, such as the use of the ankh and nemes headdress.

However, it's also true that the ancient Egyptian religion has become diluted and distorted over the years, so much so that it can be challenging to tell which traditions are real and which were added by later practitioners.

This book will help you to understand ancient Egyptian religion and magic in greater detail. It's an excellent introduction for newcomers interested in ancient Egyptian magic and experienced practitioners looking for further guidance. We'll explore what the ancient Egyptians thought about magic, the deities they worshiped and which were associated with their magical practice, and their beliefs in philosophy, cosmology, and the creation of the universe.

We'll explore the critical importance of magic not only in ancient Egyptian religion and funerary practices but also in their daily life. Many of the symbols we only know today as hieroglyphs had magical significance, and we'll look at some of the most important ones. We'll also look at the vital role that amulets and other magical tools played in Egyptian society.

This book isn't simply a scholarly overview of ancient Egyptian magical practice. We also offer easy and effective ways to incorporate ancient Egyptian magic into your daily life.

This book will help you make your own ancient Egyptian amulets and give you a better understanding of how to use other magical tools like ushabti figures. We'll also cover divination in ancient Egypt and explain how these forms of divination can be used in today's world. Furthermore, we'll look at the use of sacred plants and herbs in ancient Egyptian spell work and show you how you can use them in your magical practice.

Finally, we'll offer an overview of different types of ancient Egyptian spells and rituals. We'll offer a list of spells and rituals you can use as your starting point when incorporating ancient Egyptian magic into your life and provide instructions on how to carry out these rituals. We'll also offer ways to incorporate ancient Egyptian magic with new-age magical practices.

Chapter 1: Ancient Egyptians and Magic

Unlike the modern-day definition of magic, ancient Egyptian magic didn't involve illusions, tricks, or weird hats. Instead, it revolved around the power of the natural laws created by mystical or supernatural figures. According to ancient Egyptian beliefs, creation and existence went hand-in-hand with magic. As you will learn in the following chapter, the creation of the cosmos, the maintenance of peace, and the dynamics of daily life all involved magic. It served as a source of healing and abundance, a method of reassurance, and a guarantee of the afterlife. It touched every aspect of living, from waking up in the morning and engaging in social interactions to preparing or cooking food. Ancient Egyptians believed that their cycle of life was itself magic. Pregnancy, birth, the journey of life, death, and the concept of the afterlife were all governed by a deity who was greater and older than existence. This deity is what we know as Heka or magic.

Ancient Egyptians believed priests, pharaohs, magicians, and even people, could invoke magic through gods and goddesses. The fact that it was a vital part of healing ceremonies and rituals shows just how important magic was. Practitioners used sacred writings and spells to protect themselves against diseases, evil, and any form of danger. While magic was mainly associated with noble purposes, such as healing, protection, and as a supplement to the field of medicine, some people used it for malefic purposes like black magic and casting evil spells and curses. It was also thought that inanimate objects, like amulets and wands, could be infused with magical properties.

Heka, in a nutshell, was the deified form of magic. Some deities like Bes, Shed, Wadjet, and Tutu used it to help and protect humans. For instance, women who struggled to get pregnant were often advised to visit a Bes Chamber in a temple and spend an evening there. Ancient Egyptians thought this practice could help them conceive, which is why these rooms were often called incubation chambers. Bes was the god of fertility, childbirth, and sexuality, which is why infertile women carried the deity's amulets and had tattoos of it.

Bes was also a popular symbol of protection upon childbirth. The family of newborn children often used Bes amulets and images to protect them during childhood. These traditions were taught to them as they entered adulthood. Later, you will learn that magic and rituals were also practiced upon a person's death.

In this chapter, you will learn all about Heka and magic in ancient Egypt. Here, you will learn about the different types of magic and how it was practiced in life and upon death.

What Is Heka?

Heka is the embodiment of magic and medicine as a deity. Deified magic, or Heka, comes before any other deity in the Egyptian pantheon of gods and goddesses. The term itself means "magic" in the ancient Egyptian language. Heka was also used to refer to supernatural entities and forces, especially those who contributed to the creation of the universe and the cosmos. A literal translation of the word "Heka" would be "the usage of ka." According to ancient Egyptian religion, ka is the divine spirit or vital life force that protects an individual. It is a portion or facet of the soul of both deities and individuals. It was thought that the ka continued to live on after the person had died (a little like we think of a soul). Ancient Egyptians thought it resided in statues, icons, or pictures, which is why they built numerous statues of their rulers and deities.

Since Heka could be accessed and practiced by everyone, it could also be used for both noble and malefic purposes. This is why the term can be somewhat understood as a supernatural process to cause a desired outcome or change. Egyptologists suggest that it can also be loosely understood as a system that the ancient Egyptians used to deal with irrational or unjustifiable events and situations. In mythology, the symbol for Heka contains both serpents that Heka once defeated. There are many configurations, but they are usually either above her head or around her raised arms.

To further illustrate the significance of Heka in ancient Egyptian culture, it must be noted that ancient Egyptian physicians named themselves the "priests of Heka." Egyptians usually referred to them for help regarding magic or healing. They also consulted those physicians whenever they sought protection against disease and illnesses. Traditional medical techniques were typically supplemented with magical rites and rituals to heal patients.

You will find that numerous ancient Egyptian pharaohs, gods, and goddesses were portrayed alongside Heka flails or scepters on tablets, scarabs, and statues. Egyptian rulers and individuals of power were pictured carrying a scepter of sekhem, or power. This scepter was used to allocate terrestrial power to its carrier. You may be surprised to learn that Seichim, a modern-day healing technique similar to reiki, is derived from the word "sekhem." This scepter, however, is not to be confused with the Heka scepter, which was designed to delegate magical abilities and powers for healing purposes.

The word Heka refers to the deity and the magical practice itself. In other words, during their Heka practice, practitioners invoked Heka. This deity was first identified during the Predynastic period, and the concept was further elaborated on during the Early Dynastic Period. You will also find it in the ancient texts: Pyramid & Coffin, Intermediate Period, and the Old Kingdom.

Like Maat, the goddess (more on that later), Heka had no temples or cults. This is not because the deity lacked power but simply because the concept of Heka affected every aspect of the life of the average ancient Egyptian. When referring to Maat or Heka, it is usually the underlying concept or force being referred to.

Practitioners and Techniques

As you can probably tell by now, the creator used numerous forces, including magic, to establish the cosmos. According to ancient Egyptian lore, even symbolic behaviors can result in real or tangible outcomes. All gods and goddesses of the Egyptian pantheon were believed to possess this ability. However, their magical powers varied, as did the regulations regarding how each could put Heka into practice.

The reason why experienced priests were the primary practitioners of Heka was that they were believed to be the protectors of confidential and special information that was granted to them by the deities. This knowledge was thought to be a gift to humanity that could alleviate bad fate. Lector priests who could understand ancient magical books were the most highly esteemed practitioners of Heka. These individuals were thought to bring wax animal figures to life. Ancient Egyptians also believed that lector priests could push back the water of lakes. They also performed rituals to protect their rulers and even help reincarnate the dead. The priests who were associated with Sekhmet, the goddess of the plague, were particularly the most talented when it came to healing magic.

Scorpion charmers performed rituals to eliminate the poisonous effects of insects.
https://www.pexels.com/photo/black-and-brown-insect-with-pincers-1981542/

The scorpion charmers came next. As one can tell from the name, these practitioners used magic to eliminate the poisonous effects of insects and reptiles. Midwives, nurses, and other medical professionals were also known to incorporate magic into their practices. Amulets, which ancient Egyptians could obtain from specialized priests, were another popular source of Heka.

Ancient Egyptians mostly practiced magic at dawn. Those practicing would remain pure to enhance the magic, abstaining from sex and romantic relationships. They would also stay away from women who were menstruating and active embalmers. To add to their purity, they would bathe and wash thoroughly, wear clean clothes, and eat clean food before performing any rites.

Written magic was considered the most esteemed form of practice because very few ancient Egyptians were literate. Spells typically comprised both spoken words and physical actions. All the words needed to be pronounced correctly because only then would they activate the magic inside the amulet or the potion.

Types of Magic

As we mentioned above, there were two types of magic; protective, healing, white or benefic magic, and unfortunate, harmful, black, or malefic magic.

Besides healing and protection, white magic was often used to cast love spells, encourage conception and childbirth, accompany the deceased on their journey to the afterlife, and so on. On the other hand, black magic was typically associated with hexes, voodoo, and curses. Most deities who practiced Heka were protective gods and goddesses, meaning they practiced white or healing magic.

Amulets that were charged with white magic were used to fend off evil spirits and attract abundance or other beneficial forces. While black magic could be practiced, it was believed that whoever conducted it would face severe repercussions. Ancient Egyptians believed in the concept of karma and valued the idea of reciprocity.

Magic in Life

Wise women who were known as seers were not only able to foresee the future but also served as healing instruments. Many Egyptologists believe that these individuals were a constant aspect of spiritual belief. Seers could help with the interpretation of visions or dreams, encourage conception and childbirth, and prescribe herbal remedies. Seers were not necessarily literate. However, they, among other individuals, often memorized spells so they could use them whenever they needed to.

Ancient Egyptians of all social classes relied on Heka and magical practices in numerous aspects of their daily lives. Everyone, from rulers and esteemed members of society to enslaved people and peasants, used magic and believed in its power to change situations. Egyptologists have confirmed this information by examining the number of charms and amulets found at historical Egyptian sites. It was a very effective method of self-defense because anyone with just the right amount of knowledge could employ it in their favor. This meant that even when nurses, doctors, or priests weren't around, people could still cast their own spells and perform the appropriate rituals.

There were charms and rituals for every purpose. For instance, magic was the answer if someone needed to boost their business or productivity, overcome a challenge, beat an illness, promote fertility, or even curse their adversary. In ancient Egypt, a person's name was related to their identity. In fact, they believed that each person was granted a secret name, which was also known as "the ren." However, this name was only known by the individual and the deities. Finding out what another person's secret name was meant that this individual had been overpowered. However, discovering another person's secret name was not the only way to gain control over them. Slandering them or fully erasing their name from history was another way to do so.

Magic in Death

Heka was just as significant in death as it was in daily life. Mummification, perhaps the most popular ancient Egyptian form of magic, was practiced to preserve the deceased's body. The main idea behind mummification was to ensure that the person's soul would be able to find them in the afterlife. The priests also conducted a final ritual at the deceased's funeral. It was known as the "Opening of the Mouth Ceremony" and involved the usage of objects to touch the corpse in various places. The purpose behind this practice was to ensure that the deceased could utilize all their senses in the afterlife. They also used amulets to protect the mummies in the tomb and left practical and favored objects so they could be utilized in the afterlife.

Even if you practice modern forms of magic, it may feel impossible to wrap your head around the ancient ways of magic. This is because, over time, we've obtained a different and more enhanced understanding of the world around us. No matter how sophisticated ancient Egyptian beliefs appeared to be, they didn't necessarily depict the ultimate truth and secrets of the universe.

Chapter 2: Creation, Cosmology, and Philosophy

The ancient Egyptian myth of creation is very elaborate, like other tales and fables. It is no surprise that there are numerous renditions of the Egyptian tale of how the cosmos came into existence. In essence, it was believed that the gods responsible for the world's creation were the ones who dictated the flow of nature, the societal structures, and the basic principles of life. The myth of creation is found in ancient texts, buildings, scrolls, tombs, and temples. The tale recounts how the god Atum managed to create the Earth out of nothing but chaos. This is why they held the Earth in the highest regard, trusting that it was a sacred place that mirrored the home of the gods in the sky.

According to the ancient Egyptians, the creation of the cosmos was not an overnight job. Instead, they thought the universe was created over extended periods when the gods resided on Earth. Each of them built kingdoms on the foundations of justice and passed it onto the rightful Pharoah when it was time to return to the sky.

The Egyptian Book of the Dead explains that the god of Heliopolis, Atum, was the one behind the creation of the universe. It recounts that the world was nothing but a vast space of darkness and waters that flowed without direction. It was known as "Nun." Nun embodied a total of 4 pairs of both female and male deities. Each pair symbolized one of the 4 Nun principles, which are infinite water, invisibility, darkness, and a diminished sense of direction.

The creation of the universe started when Atum created himself out of nothingness. He used his name's power and will to emerge out of Nun. He was thenceforth known as the creator of all deities and humans and was charged with instilling order on Earth and in the sky (or heavens). Atum was the ruler of the Heavens and Earth, which is why he held the symbol of life known as the ankh. Atum carried a scepter wherever he went, the symbol of authority within the monarchy, and he is depicted with that along with the double crown.

In this chapter, we will uncover the ancient Egyptian myth of creation. We will also delve deep into the ancient Egyptian worldview, spiritual beliefs, and the concept of the afterlife. By the end, you will have grasped an understanding of philosophies like the 7 Maat principles and the idea of heart-weighing before Aaru.

The Ancient Egyptian Myth of Creation

The stories recounted on the walls of the Pyramids suggest that Atum created himself out of darkness and chaos and arose as a Bennu bird. When the sun rose, Atum took flight, traveling from Heliopolis, and landing on an obelisk (Benben) – the representation of the sun's light. He became engulfed in fire after building a nest of branches and herbs. In most pyramids, and with some obelisks, you will see a capstone at the peak. This stone symbolizes rebirth, renewal, and everlasting life.

At the start of creation, Atum created twins, a son and a daughter. The son, Shu, represents the arid air around us, and the daughter, Tefnut, represents the moist air. Together, they represented life and justice, or right, the two universal fundamental principles of human existence. They were also responsible for parting the heavens from the water. Shu and Tefnut became parents, bringing Nut and Geb into the world. Nut represents the sky, and Geb represents the land (dry land). When the primordial waters receded (Nut), an earthy mound was revealed (Geb). This gave way to the first piece of solid dry land where Re, the sun god, was finally able to rest. Atum was referred to as Re during the ancient Egyptian dynastic period. The title Re alluded to the first rising of the sun.

Together, Geb and Nut created four children; the god of order, Osiris, the god of disorder, Seth, and Isis and Nephthys, their sisters. The offspring of Geb and Nut gave way to a whole new generation that finally contributed to the cessation of the Heliopolitan Ennead. This Ennead was made up of nine deities, starting with Atum.

As we mentioned above, the myth of creation is recounted in several ways. One story tells of the Heliopolitan Ennead being replaced with the Ogdoad, utilizing a group of eight gods. The Ogdoad consisted of 4 pairs of male and female deities representing primeval chaos and all its aspects. The gods were portrayed as frogs and the goddesses as snakes. The names of the deities that symbolized water were Nun and Naunet. Amun and Amaunet personified the principle of invisibility or hiddenness. Heh and Huahet combine to represent infinity, while Ket and Kauket represent darkness.

The Eye of Re, the Sun God

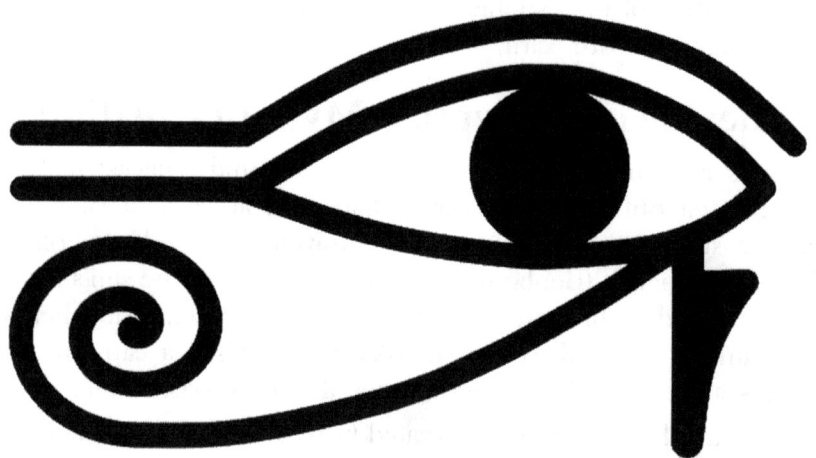

The eye of Re depicts the power to see, shed light, and take action.
Polyester,fi:Käyttäjä:kompak, CC BY-SA 3.0 <http://creativecommons.org/licenses/by-sa/3.0/>, via Wikimedia Commons: https://commons.wikimedia.org/wiki/File:Eye_of_Ra.svg

Re, the sun god, governed the Earth. At that period, the land was where both divine bodies and humans existed peacefully. According to mythology, Re's eye was responsible for the creation of humanity. This is why the eye of Re was also known as Wedjat, which means the eye of wholeness. Humankind was born from Re's eye when it became separated from his body. Shu and Tefnut both tried to catch it, but they were unable, and the tears were shed through the struggle, humans forming from those tears.

Atum is often depicted as an eye, the symbol popular with many deities, including Re and Horus (the son of Osiris and Isis). The eye of Re is also a depiction of the power to see, shed light, and take action. Returning the eye to its owner, the creator, would be a symbol of healing for the Earth. It meant that essential constructs such as order and justice would again be restored to the land. Maintaining these principles meant stopping chaos from spreading on Earth. Keeping the peace was an essential role of the Pharaoh.

The alternative version to this story suggests that when the Wedjat decided to leave, Re asked the moon god, Thoth, to bring it back. He went to fetch it only to find that another eye had replaced the one that had wandered off. Normally, the original eye was furious, so Re decided to place it on his brow. However, he shaped it into a cobra goddess known as the uraeus, so it could rule the entire universe. Ever since that happened, the pharaohs placed the symbol of the cobra goddess on their brows to symbolize protection. The placement of the uraeus also showed that they were Re's descendants.

The Outburst of Rebellion

When Re grew older, the deities avidly used his softening brain and growing confusion. It was also believed that humans, too, tried to take advantage of his condition. This caused them to fall out of divine grace. Re, being the great god he was, didn't stay silent in the face of rebellion. He sent his eye out to slaughter those who turned against him. He shapeshifted into Sekhmet, the powerful female deity who took the form of a lioness to punish his adversaries. When he had finished, he transformed into the goddess Hathor who appeared as a cow.

Although he won, Re was worn down by his pain and worries. He decided to flee the world, still taking the shape of Hathor. Hathor ascended to the heavens above, riding atop Nut (the sky). Those deities who clung to Hathor's stomach went with him, and they became the stars in the night sky. The moon watches over us, and that is because Thoth (the moon god) was given magic to protect humans. At this point, the heavens and the mortal realm, people and gods, split.

The Journey of Re

Re took to the skies, birthed each morning to journey from each other to the west. He used a boat (known as the Bark of Millions of Years), and a few other gods also joined him to help. Khepri, the scarab god, carried Re across the sky. Apep, his main enemy, was a huge serpent that resided in the Nile. The Nile River was believed to be the waters of the Nun. Although Apep continuously tried to block the boat's passage, Re always emerged victorious.

As you can tell by now, Re was the most significant deity in the entire pantheon of Egyptian gods. He had numerous names and titles, including Aten, which meant the sun disk, and Khepri, meaning the rising sun. At the sun's height or zenith, he was known as the scarab, and his most popular name, Re, referred to his role as the supreme god of Heliopolis. The deity was also known as Atum at sunset.

Obelisks, the sphinx, and the pyramids all relate closely to Re. When the sun rose, it looked like it was winged, and this winged journeyman (or journey-god) was depicted as Re-Horakhty. At some point in history, this god was symbolized by the sphinx. The scarab also symbolized Re because it buried its eggs in a hole where they hatched like the sun god pushed out the sun from the eastern horizon.

Worldview and Spiritual Beliefs

Ancient Egyptians were polytheistic, which meant that they believed in the existence of several gods. They believed that each deity had unique characteristics and capabilities, as well as a distinct nature. Like other polytheistic religions, the deities of the ancient Egyptians neither had unending power nor limitless knowledge. They were still much more powerful than the average human being and nearly immortal. Ancient Egyptian deities could also normally survive fatal blows or wounds, managed to be present in more than one place at a single time, and could impact people in both visible and invisible ways. Most deities were benevolent. However, one couldn't always count on their favors. This is why people always had to ensure that their deities were appeased and satisfied.

Unfortunately, the traits and characteristics of each deity were not always strictly known. Many of them, however, had primary associations. For instance, Re was linked to the sun, and Hathor was associated with women. It's worth noting that there were a lot of overlapping features between major gods, though. It could also be observed that the deities with more restricted characteristics had the least power. As you may recall, a single god or mythological figure could go by more than one name. The three main social classes of deities were males, females, and younger deities.

Gods were generally associated with certain geographical locations. Heliopolis, Memphis, is the original location of the sun cult, and the cult is related to Ptah, Thebes, and Amon. They also had main manifestations and typically corresponded to at least one animal species. As for the gods, the bull and the falcon were the most significant figures. The female deities were usually associated with lionesses, cows, vultures, and cobras. Some deities, however, had specific associations. Sebek, for example, was linked to the crocodile. Thoth corresponded to two animals; the baboon and the ibis.

Ka, which refers to the vital energy or life force of a human, was transferred from one generation to the following one. The "ba" is the force that enables us to move freely and appear in different forms. This force was mainly associated with the next world. Your "akh" is your spirit once it has left this world for the next.

Gods often took the form of humans. Some of them only showed up in human form (Min and Ptah especially). They would also appear as part human and part animal, taking the head of the animal associated with them. The sphinx is an exception, where the human and animal parts are switched. Sphinxes were also often depicted with other heads, such as that of a falcon or a ram.

The ancient Egyptian religion lasted for over 3000 years. Egyptians were very spiritual, and their religion was incorporated into numerous aspects of their lives. They always aimed to provide for their deities, ensure their satisfaction, and obtain their favor. The ancient Egyptian spiritual beliefs were very intricate and complex. This intricacy could be observed through the various manifestations of the deities and the numerous mythological roles they assumed. The Egyptian pantheon comprised deities who played major roles in the world. The building would also house some of the minor deities and some demons, foreign deities, and mortals (mainly dead kings).

The religious practices and rituals mainly revolved around the ruler of the country or its Pharaoh. The chosen ones, the pharaohs, were believed to have the power of the gods running through their veins, and their blood was sacred. They were chosen to maintain order in the mortal realm and could also help to bridge the boundary between humans and deities - temples would be built, rituals performed, and the deities would be revered. These Pharaohs were believed to be of the gods themselves, descending from the deities, thus able to commune with them the best. People could pray or use magic to interact directly with the gods. Over time, the power of the Pharaohs declined. This meant that personal spiritual practices held more meaning, substance, and power.

Cosmology

The ancient Egyptian universe was mainly built on the 7 principles of Maat. These principles hold numerous meanings and cannot be translated into English. They can be roughly translated to represent order, truth, justice, and virtue. Maat was everlasting and fixed. It could never be changed because the world would cease to exist without it. As anyone would expect, numerous threats - especially ones related to chaos and a lack of order- faced society. This meant that their society had to come together and make the effort needed to maintain Maat. It was believed to be replenished by recurrent events, including the annual flooding of the Nile river. It was thought that this event mirrored the start of creation.

Interestingly, ancient Egyptians believed that the Earth was flat. Geb represented the land, and his sister Nut represented the sky - in the middle was Shu, the air. Below Geb was a parallel universe that comprised the underworld and the undersky. Nu, the chaos that came before all creation, existed beyond the skies. Duat referred to a mysterious place that was linked to death and rebirth. This was the area that Ra journeyed through every day.

The Seven Maat Principles

The goddess Maat exhibited the principles of Maat - harmony, balance, justice, truth, reciprocity, order, and propriety. It was believed that all members of society, especially the Pharaohs and their relatives, should embody or follow those principles. By allowing Maat to govern every aspect of life, including how people deal with others and how they act and behave, harmony and peace could be achieved. People who neglected these principles were considered outlaws, and the rulers who Maat did not guide were believed to be unfit for their role.

The truth refers to a person's ability to differentiate between what is real and what isn't. People who lived their truth behaved in a way that favored the greater good. The truth refers to the belief that all living beings are sacred and deserving of respect. Justice was associated with not only social equity but equity between nature and all living beings. Rulers were expected to be just and had to ensure that the basic needs of everyone were met.

Harmony refers to the state in which all living beings interact and align beautifully with one another. It was related to authenticity and freedom of expression. The state of balance refers to when a person's internal and external environments align. Order was associated with organization and clarity.

Reciprocity is quite similar to the concept of karma. Your actions, whether good or bad, will be met with the appropriate reward or consequence. In other words, "What goes around comes around." Finally, propriety was the expectation that a person would do whatever was right. It meant a person should not hurt a living being, including themselves.

The Afterlife

Ancient Egyptians believed that the ka, or a person's life-force energy, continued to live on even after an individual's death. Since they were very concerned with an individual's fate following their death, they built tombs and provided food offerings to the deceased. It was also believed that the ba, or a person's spiritual traits, also lived on. This is why they conducted funeral rites to ensure the release of the ba so it could rejoin the ka. They were both expected to live on as akh. They practiced mummification techniques to preserve the deceased's body because they thought the ba returned to the body each night.

A ritual was conducted to determine where the soul of the deceased would go. Those who had passed would arrive in Maat's great hall, and it is there where their heart would be weighed. They would face Ren and the forty-two judges and have all their sins told to them. Once they had listened to all of their sins, their heart would be weighed. The heart was weighed against a feather to determine if it was heavy with sin or pure and light. If balanced with the feather, the individual was allowed to enter Aaru or heaven. If it was heavier, their soul was thought to have been destroyed forever.

Like in numerous ancient and modern-day cultures, traditions, and religions, the sun was a highly significant entity in ancient Egyptian culture. This symbol of renewal and light never failed to illuminate the vast lands of Egypt. It makes sense that the ancient Egyptians believed it to be the best-fitting symbol for the creator of the entire world. Where there is no sun, there is no life.

Chapter 3: Major Female Deities

One of the many fascinating aspects of Ancient Egyptian culture was their deities. Religion was a big part of ancient Egypt, and it was incorporated into various areas of their lives. Consequently, their deities were held in very high regard, and they constantly appeased them by presenting them with offerings and performing certain rituals. The ancient Egyptians were polytheistic since they worshiped more than one deity. There were various gods and goddesses in their culture. Female deities were highly respected as women played a vital role in society and were treated equally to their male counterparts. This chapter will focus on major female deities in ancient Egypt.

Isis, Goddess of Magic and Healing

Isis, goddess of magic and healing.
Jeff Dahl, CC BY-SA 4.0 <https://creativecommons.org/licenses/by-sa/4.0>, via Wikimedia Commons: https://commons.wikimedia.org/wiki/File:Isis.svg

Hieroglyphic Name

Isis was called ꜣst in ancient Egypt. The name translates to "female of the throne," which refers to her being the "queen of the throne." This is clear from her illustrations which featured a throne emblem on her head. Her name also indicated her prominent role as a royal deity. Since the ancient Egyptians omitted vowels, it is hard to know exactly how her name was pronounced. However, after further research, it is believed that her name was pronounced as ooh-saht.

Worshiping Isis

Isis wasn't only worshiped in ancient Egypt. After Alexander the Great conquered the country, more people became aware of the goddess, and the number of her worshippers grew. The ancient Greeks associated Isis with their goddess of agriculture, Demeter, while the ancient Romans linked her to their goddess of love, Venus. There were people in Asia, Britain, Israel, Turkey, Afghanistan, and Syria who also worshiped the goddess. Various temples throughout the Mediterranean were built in her honor to appease her. To this day, there are still pagans who revere Isis.

Symbols
- Throne
- Cow's horns and solar disk
- The knot of Isis (an ancient Egyptian symbol that means life)
- Sistrum rattle (a musical instrument that wards off evil spirits)
- Wings

Correspondences
- Fertility
- Motherhood
- Magic
- Rebirth
- Healing
- Death
- Water
- The color green

Myth

Isis was married to Osiris, the god of the underworld. Osiris and Isis wanted to help mankind become more civilized. Isis worked with her husband to better educate Egyptian women so they could live and thrive. Seth, who was Isis and Osiris's brother and the god of disorder, murdered Osiris so that he himself could become king. Isis didn't know what had happened to her husband, and she looked for him everywhere. When she found him and brought his body back to Egypt, Seth dismembered him and scattered the pieces worldwide. Loyal and devoted, Isis didn't give up and transformed into a bird to look for her husband's parts. With the help of her sister Nephthys, they found Osiris's parts and put them back together. Using her magic, Isis made her husband whole again, but he was a mummy, neither living nor dead. Other gods were impressed by Isis's devotion and determination to find her husband.

Connecting with Isis

If you want to connect with Isis, you should build an altar for her in your home. It is really simple. Just choose an undisturbed area and hang a picture or place a statue of her and light a candle. Since she is associated with the color green, you can also plant a small garden and dedicate it to her.

Offerings
- Sunflowers
- Daisies
- Lotus
- Red roses
- White roses
- Milk
- Wine
- Cinnamon oil
- Jasmine oil
- Sandalwood oil
- Honey
- Peanuts
- Grapes
- Chocolate
- Coconuts
- Moonstone
- Diamond
- Gold
- Pearl
- Anything green, gold, blue, red, and white

Signs Isis Is Calling You

Isis may appear in your dreams, or you may hear or see her name on TV or online. You may have the urge to work with the sun and moon. Kites and cows will start showing up in your daily life. You may receive one of her symbols as a gift. You will see them in dreams or in reality.

The Experience of Connecting with Isis

Many women have found ways to connect with Isis. The goddess usually calls to all women, specifically mothers and widows. When they answer her call, she can help them follow their intuition, learn to trust, and heal, and she can also provide guidance.

Maat, the Goddess of Justice and Truth

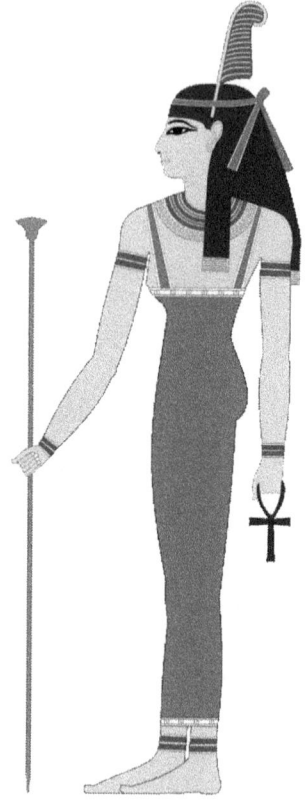

Maat, goddess of justice and truth.
No machine-readable author provided. Jeff Dahl assumed (based on copyright claims)., CC BY-SA 4.0 <https://creativecommons.org/licenses/by-sa/4.0>, via Wikimedia Commons: https://commons.wikimedia.org/wiki/File:Maat.svg

Hieroglyphic Name

Maat was spelled m3ʔt in ancient Egyptian. The name means "That which is straight," which refers to justice, harmony, and order.

Worshiping Maat

Maat was worshiped all over ancient Egypt. However, we can say that she was and still is worshiped worldwide. Maat was considered a concept rather than a real deity. She didn't represent justice. She is justice, truth, and harmony. Since many people have lived by these concepts to this day, it is easy to assume that we all follow Maat's principles.

Symbols
- Ostrich feather
- Ankh (key of life)
- Scepter
- Wings
- Scales
- Turquoise

Correspondences
- Cosmic order
- Harmony
- Truth
- Justice

Myth

Maat played a huge role in ancient Egyptian mythology. She was the daughter of Ra, the creator deity and the god of the sun. Maat was born at the same moment Ra created the world. Her essence was infused with the universe, and all creation has lived according to her principles ever since. She brought comic order to an empty and chaotic world. The concept of Maat was represented in various Egyptian myths. Maat played a role in the story of Isis. She and her twin sister Nephthys represented life and death, respectively. Nephthys wasn't evil, but both sisters balanced each other just like lightness and darkness. In other words, they both represented comic balance, Maat.

Connecting with Maat

Guided meditation is one of the best ways to connect you with Maat. It is recommended that you hold a white feather in your hand while meditating.

- Find a quiet spot and sit in a comfortable position.
- Close your eyes and visualize yourself entering a holy chamber in an ancient Egyptian temple.
- Maat welcomes you with scales in her hands.
- You place your heart on her scale.
- Maat will weigh your heart against the feather of truth.

- If your heart is heavier than a feather, Maat will tell you what negative emotion is consuming your heart, like anger, envy, resentment, ... etc.
- If you are willing to release these emotions, she will place her hand over your heart, and a divine white light will shine from it through your heart.
- Your heart will be lighter than a feather.
- She will place your heart in your chest.
- She will ask you to replace all the negative emotions you released with positive ones like love, compassion, and forgiveness.

Offerings
- Chicken
- Fish
- Cold water
- Eggplant
- Olive oil
- Tea with milk
- Vinegar
- Hummus
- Almonds
- Scales
- Gold jewelry
- Clear quartz
- White marble
- Wine
- Fragrant incense

Signs Maat Is Calling You

Maat may appear in your dreams, or you may hear or come across her name in various places, like on TV or in a book. White feathers may begin showing up in your life.

The Experience of Connecting with Maat

People usually call on Maat when there is chaos and instability in their lives. Her followers usually experience harmony afterward as she brings unity and balance back into their lives.

Bastet, Goddess of Cats and Protection

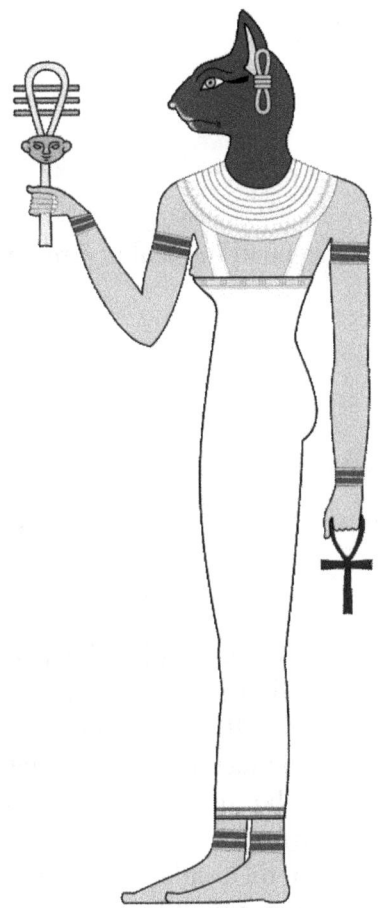

Bastet, goddess of cats and protection.
Gunawan Kartapranata, CC BY-SA 3.0 <https://creativecommons.org/licenses/by-sa/3.0>, via Wikimedia Commons: https://commons.wikimedia.org/wiki/File:Bastet.svg

Hieroglyphic Name

Bastet was spelled bꜣstt in ancient Egyptian. Historians believe she used to be called Bast, "soul of Auset." Auset was another name for Bastet's mother, Isis. Egyptian priests later changed her name to Bastet, which means "She of the ointment jar." For this reason, her name is written with the Hieroglyphic symbol for an ointment jar.

Worshiping Bastet

Bastet was worshiped all over Egypt, specifically in Lower Egypt. The Greeks linked her to the goddess Artemis, and she became the goddess of the moon. There are still people who worship Bastet, and her cults are alive and active in several countries. Nowadays, Bastet followers worship her as the goddess of fertility.

Symbols
- Cats
- Lioness
- Solar disk
- Sistrum (ancient Egyptian musical instrument)
- Ointment Jar

Correspondences
- Fertility
- Home
- Childbirth
- Women's secrets
- Domesticity

Myth

Prince Setna, King Rameses' son, stole The Book of Thoth, a magic book written by Thoth, the god of knowledge and writing. One day, Setna saw a very beautiful woman and offered her money to sleep with her. The woman, called Tabubu, was the daughter of a Bastet priest. She agreed to have an affair with the prince, but he had to be discreet because she was a lady of ranking. When arriving to meet the prince, Tabubu had one condition before they began their affair. He had to sign over to her everything he owned. Setna, consumed by lust, agreed and made the deal right away.

Tabubu changed into a robe that showcased all her beautiful physical features to entice Setna. She made another condition that he had to sign over his children's possessions, and he obliged. She made one last request that Setna should kill his children. He agreed and gave the order right away. As Setna approached Tabubu and touched her, she screamed very loudly and disappeared.

Tabubu wasn't the daughter of a priest but a manifestation of the goddess Bastet. She was punishing Setna for angering the gods and stealing the Book of Thoth. However, Bastet wasn't so cruel. There is a version of this story where Setna repented after he lost everything and returned The Book of Thoth. When he arrived home, his children were alive and well.

Connecting with Bastet

Building an altar under the goddess's name will help you connect with her. Decorate the altar with rattles, baskets, brightly colored crystals, and pictures of lions and cats. Offering a prayer through singing and dancing will also help you connect with the deity. For pregnant women or those who hope to get pregnant and require Bastet protection, you can make an offering.

Offerings
- Chocolate
- Honey
- Perfumed ointment
- Milk
- Statues of cats
- Raw meat
- Catnip herbs
- Wine

Signs Bastet Is Calling You

The cat goddess will call on you using her favorite pet. Cats may follow you, and you may see them wherever you go. You may feel connected to a stray cat and may even adopt it. A friend may give you a gift with a cat image on it, or you randomly open a book and you land on a cat picture. Bastet may also appear in your dreams. You may also hear meowing when there are no cats around or simply feel the goddess's presence.

The Experience of Connecting with Bastet

Bastet followers believe that the goddess is always watching over their cats. When they connect with her, they feel that their cats are being protected.

Sekhmet, Goddess of War

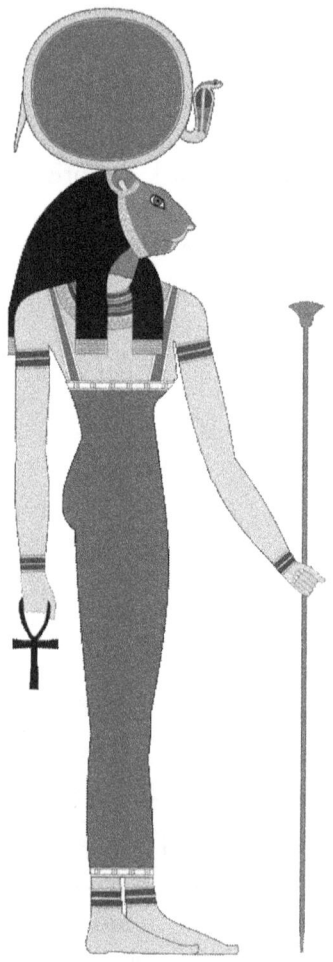

Sekhmet, goddess of war.
FDRMRZUSA, CC BY-SA 4.0 <https://creativecommons.org/licenses/by-sa/4.0>, via Wikimedia Commons: https://commons.wikimedia.org/wiki/File:Sekhmet_mirror.svg

Hieroglyphic Name

Sekhmet is pronounced ˈsɛkˌmɛt. It comes from the word "Sekhem," which means "powerful." Sekhmet means "She who is powerful."

Worshiping Sekhmet

Sekhmet was worshiped in Egypt in the Delta, Luxor, Letopolis, and Memphis. She is still highly revered and worshiped to this day, as many people consider her one of the most prominent pagan deities.

Symbols
- Red linen
- Lioness
- Sun disk
- Ankh
- Blood
- Fire
- Desert
- Red, orange, and yellow crystals
- The colors gold, red, and orange

Correspondences
- Healers
- Healing
- Medicine
- Chaos
- War
- Plague
- Hot desert

Myth

Sekhmet was Ra's daughter, who he created from fire. He became angry with mankind because they weren't following Maat's principles. So, he sent his daughter Sekhmet to punish them. To Ra's surprise, Sekhmet was hungry for blood and caused carnage. Egypt was covered in blood. When Ra saw the state of his people, he repented for his actions. He ordered Sekhmet to stop immediately. However, the goddess wouldn't listen to him as she was consumed with bloodlust. Ra decided to take action to save his people. He poured thousands of bear jugs and permanganate juice into Sekhmet's path. She thought it was blood and consumed all of it. She was so drunk that she passed out for three days.

There are two versions of this story's ending. One said that when she woke up, she was calm, and her bloodthirst was gone. Another said that when she opened her eyes, she saw Ptah, the god of creation. She fell in love with him right away. As she was the goddess of war and chaos and he was the god of creation, their union brought back Maat (balance). She gave birth to a son, Nefertum, who became the god of healing. When

Matt was established, humanity was saved.

Connecting with Sekhmet

You can connect with Sekhmet through meditation. Light a candle, use some incense, sit in a comfortable position in a quiet spot, and close your eyes.

- Take a few deep breaths and relax your body.
- Set your intention, in your head or out loud, to connect with Sekhmet.
- Imagine you are in a desert on a very hot summer day.
- You see the pyramids far away, and you walk toward them.
- It isn't an easy journey since the sun is blazing hot.
- You arrive and walk into the middle pyramid.
- It is quiet inside, with beautiful paintings and symbols.
- You find a door, and it slides open for you.
- A voice comes from the inside saying, "enter."
- There is a beautiful woman sitting on a throne who asks you who you are.
- You tell her your name and that you are here to connect with Sekhmet.
- She nods and informs you that she is Sekhmet.
- There is silence in the room.
- Moments later, the goddess stands up and begins talking to you.
- Listen to what she is saying, ask questions, and connect with her.
- When you have finished your conversation, she will leave the room.
- Take a few deep breaths, and then open your eyes.

You can also connect with her by creating an altar indoors or outdoors and decorating it with her symbols.

Offerings

- Music
- Food
- Drinks
- Burning incense

Signs Sekhmet Is Calling You

Sekhmet may call on you by appearing to you in your dreams. You may also see her symbols in your dreams or reality. If you are focused, you might feel her guidance.

The Experience of Connecting with Sekhmet

People usually call on Sekhmet when they need courage and strength to speak up or stand up for themselves. When they connect with her, they feel strong, empowered, and able to speak their truth.

Serqet, Goddess of the Dead and Healing Stings

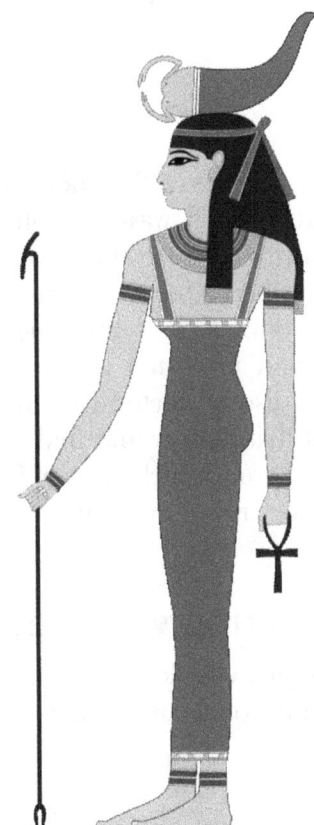

Serqet, goddess of the dead and healing stings.
Jeff Dahl, CC BY-SA 4.0 <https://creativecommons.org/licenses/by-sa/4.0>, via Wikimedia Commons: https://commons.wikimedia.org/wiki/File:Serket.svg

Hieroglyphic Name

Serqet is pronounced ˈsɜːrˌkɛt. Her name means "She who causes the throat to breathe." This refers to her ability to cure snakes and scorpion stings.

Worshiping Serqet

Serqet was mainly worshiped in Lower Egypt.

Symbols

- The Ankh
- The Was Scepter (a Hieroglyphic symbol for power)
- Scorpions

Correspondences

- Magic
- Healing
- Protection

Myth

Serqet was one of the goddesses of the underworld. Ra would travel to the underworld every night, which wasn't a safe journey. The goddess would watch over him and make sure there weren't any dangers in his path. There was a serpent called Apep, who was an evil spirit that caused destruction. He was also one of Ra's arch-enemies. Serqet restrained Apep in the underworld and protected anyone journeying through the underworld from him. She also protected Isis when she gave birth to her son Horus. Isis was afraid that Seth would find them and her husband's fate would befall her son. Serqet watched over Isis when she was giving birth and kept Horus safe. In so many ways, Serqet is considered a protector.

Connecting with Serqet

You can connect with Serqet by building an altar in her name. You can decorate the altar with the key to life and images or statues of the goddess.

Offerings

- Bloodstone crystal
- Citrine
- Amethyst
- Garnet

- Cayenne pepper
- Angelica root
- Cannabis
- Cinnamon
- Anything in gold, purple, or red

Signs Serqet Is Calling You

Similar to the various goddesses we have already mentioned, Serqet may appear to you in your dreams, or you may feel her presence around you.

The Experience of Connecting with Serqet

People who are recovering from substance abuse call on Serqet for her detoxification and healing abilities. It is believed that Serqet gives them strength through these hard times. Usually, when we are at our weakest, we look for a higher power to help get us out of adversity. Serqet is a protector and a healer who can give you the support you need.

Neith Goddess of War and Creation

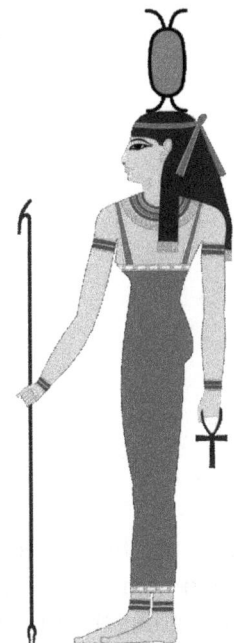

Neith, goddess of war and creation.
Jeff Dahl, CC BY-SA 4.0 <https://creativecommons.org/licenses/by-sa/4.0>, via Wikimedia Commons: https://commons.wikimedia.org/wiki/File:Neith.svg

Hieroglyphic Name

Neith's original name is believed to have been Nrt which means "She, the terrifying one," since she was one of the most powerful deities.

Worshiping Neith

Neith was worshiped all over Egypt, but her most loyal followers were in Lower Egypt.

Symbols

- Sword
- Shield
- Bow and arrow
- Weaving shuttle
- Red crown of Lower Egypt
- Ankh
- Scepter
- Spider
- Cows

Correspondences

- War
- Wisdom
- Creation
- Weaving
- Water and rivers
- The cosmos
- Mothers
- Hunting
- Childbirth
- Fate

Myth

When Isis's son Horus grew up, he was ready to take his place as the rightful king of Egypt. He argued with Ra and the assembly of gods that, as Osiris's son, he should be king rather than his uncle Seth. Naturally, Seth opposed it. When Ra heard both sides, he felt that Horus wasn't ready to be king. He was young and didn't have enough experience. However, the other gods were on Horus's side.

The gods couldn't make a decision, so they enlisted the help of the wisest deity, Neith. She decided that Horus was the rightful king and should take his place on the throne. However, she was still fair and compensated Seth with two wives.

Connecting with Neith

You can build an altar for Neith indoors or outdoors. Decorate it with images or statues of the goddesses. You can also add ankhs, a small bow and an arrow, and toy cows and spiders.

Offerings
- Cool water
- Bread
- Dates
- Onions

Signs Neith Is Calling You

You may either have a dream or a vision of Neith. You may also start seeing her symbols in your daily life. For instance, a spider may crawl into your backyard when you don't have spiders in your area, or you will see a cow a few times on your way to work. You may also see a red crown, sword, or shield or be given the key to life as a gift.

The Experience of Connecting with Neith

People who have connected with Neith have mentioned how motherly and protective she was.

There are so many things that we can learn from female Egyptian deities. Just keep your heart, eyes, and mind open as one may be calling out to you. If not, connect with them using the methods we have covered here.

Chapter 4: Major Male Deities

Now that you have learned about the major female deities in ancient Egypt, we will take a look at the male gods. Male deities are as prominent in Egyptian mythology as their female counterparts. Their lives are filled with fascinating stories that can help you not only learn about their characteristics but also know which deity you can call on when you need guidance.

Ra, the Creator and the God of the Sun

Ra, the creator and god of the sun.
Jeff Dahl, CC BY-SA 4.0 <https://creativecommons.org/licenses/by-sa/4.0>, via Wikimedia Commons: https://commons.wikimedia.org/wiki/File:Re-Horakhty.svg

Hieroglyphic Name

Ra was called rꜥ in ancient Egypt, and it is pronounced rɑː. The name means "sun." He also went by multiple other names; Atum, Khepri, Ra-Horakhty, Re, Pra, and Amun-Re. Ra also had another name that no one was allowed to learn since it was the secret to his divine power. When Isis tried to find out his secret name, he revealed some of his other names but not the ones she wanted to know. He said, "I am Khepera in the morning, Ra at noon-day, and Temu in the evening," which gave us an idea of some of the deity's other names.

Worshiping Ra

Ra was worshiped all over ancient Egypt. It is believed that his worship began in an Egyptian town called Iunu in Northern Cairo. When the Greeks conquered Egypt, they named the town Heliopolis, which means "city of the sun of god." Thousands of years later, the city of Heliopolis is still standing, and its name remains unchanged. Ra is still revered, and some people worship him and believe he has always been the supreme god since he created the world.

Symbols

- Solar disk
- Scepter
- Ankh
- The sun
- Scarab beetle
- Falcon
- Boat
- Eye of Ra
- Ram
- Lion
- Cobra

Correspondences

- The sun
- Creation
- Earth
- Heaven
- The underworld

- The sky
- Balance
- Destruction
- Justice
- Royalty
- Healing
- Vengeance
- Vitality
- Prosperity
- Protection
- Enlightenment

Myth

Before the world was created, there was only darkness. The only thing that existed was water which was called Nun. Ra created himself out of Nun. According to one version of this legend, he was able to bring himself to life by uttering his own name, and, in another version, he came into existence by an effort of will. Next came the twins: Tefnut and Shu. The world was still dark since there was no sunlight or moonlight, so Ra could not find his children. Consequently, Ra created an eye to help him look for his new children. The eye left to find the new gods, but it discovered an unpleasant surprise when it returned. Ra had created another eye in its absence.

The first eye was very angry and felt betrayed. Ra made the first eye stronger than the second to quell its rage. The stronger of the two transformed into the sun, and the weaker transformed into the moon. For this reason, the sun was referred to as "the eye of Ra." After that, Ra created celestial bodies, gods, and goddesses. There are various stories about how Ra created humanity. One story says that he wept after creating the gods and his tears became mankind. Another story says that he created the world by uttering everything by its secret name. While there is a story that says after the first eye discovered that Ra created a second one, it cried out of rage, and in another version, it cried out of loneliness, and its tears became humanity.

The one thing that all these stories share in common is that humanity was created out of loneliness, anger, and misery. In many ways, this story is a similar interpretation of mankind and the condition of the world, which has remained unchanged for centuries.

Connecting with Ra

As mentioned, building an altar is one of the most effective methods to help you connect with a deity. Simply choose a small space in your home, like a shelf or a table. Place images, statues, or crystals related to Ra or ancient Egypt. You can also add candles or incense. Since Ra is the god of the sun, the best times to connect with him are at sunrise, sunset, and high noon. So cast your spells, and practice yoga or meditation at these times.

Offerings
- Water
- Frankincense
- Candlelight
- Beer
- Bread
- Fruit
- Poultry
- Gold
- Linen

Signs Ra Is Calling You

As mentioned in the previous chapters, gods usually call on us in our dreams either by appearing themselves or sending us their symbols. You may see the sun, a falcon, or a scarab beetle in your dreams. You may also hear the name Ra or keep finding things related to the sun in dreams or reality. For instance, a friend may give you a sun necklace, or you may keep finding posts about the Sun or Ra online.

The Experience of Connecting with Ra

Ra's followers often call on him when they need balance in their lives since he is the god of creation and destruction. Ra also protects people who seek justice, like judges, juries, lawyers, police officers, etc.

Osiris, the God of Life and Death

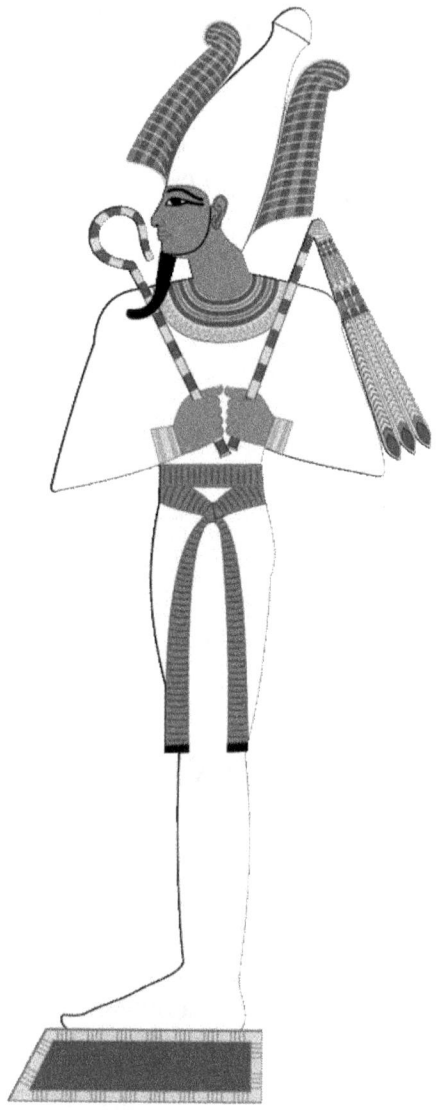

Osiris, god of life and death.
Jeff Dahl, CC BY-SA 4.0 <https://creativecommons.org/licenses/by-sa/4.0>, via Wikimedia Commons: https://commons.wikimedia.org/wiki/File:Standing_Osiris_edit1.svg

Hieroglyphic Name

Osiris used to be called wsjr in hieroglyphic, which was pronounced as jsjrj because hieroglyphs didn't have any vowels. Egyptologists later changed the vocalization of the name to Usir, which is pronounced as "oos-ee-r."

Osiris is the Greek version of the name. The name translates to "powerful" or "mighty," which makes it an appropriate name for one of the most prominent gods in ancient Egypt.

Worshiping Osiris

Many people worshiped Osiris throughout ancient Egypt, and his main followers were from Abydos, an ancient city in Upper Egypt. He was the god of death, and the ancient Egyptians believed in life after death, so Osiris was regarded as a deity who could grant life after death. As a result, he was revered in other places worldwide, like Rome and Greece. The Greeks associated him with their own god of the underworld, Hades.

Symbols
- Mummy gauze
- Crook and flail (symbols of royalty)
- Green skin
- Atef crown (feathered white crown)
- Ostrich feathers
- Djed (represents power and stability)

Correspondences
- The underworld
- Death
- Strength
- Fertility
- Agriculture
- Resurrection
- Flood
- The cycle of the Nile

Myth

We mentioned Osiris in the previous chapter. He was Isis's husband, who his brother Seth killed and dismembered. Osiris became the god of the underworld when Isis brought him back. He was a mummy, neither dead nor alive. However, before he became the god of the underworld, he was the god of agriculture. Legend has it that the ancient Egyptians used to be cannibals until Osiris introduced agriculture to them. That said, historians argue that this myth is lacking, and there is no real evidence to support it. Still, Osiris is credited for bringing agriculture, order, and civilization to a chaotic and uncivilized world.

Looking at illustrations of Osiris, you will see that he was depicted with a kind smile. This shows that he was a good and approachable god. The people loved and respected him and didn't fear him like other gods. He only wanted to help mankind. When he became the god of the underworld, he made sure that justice and order prevailed.

Connecting with Osiris

Building an altar for Osiris will help you connect with him. Decorate the altar with images or statues of the god or by using any of his symbols like the crook and flail or the Atef crown. You can also try visualization and meditation while holding an ostrich feather if you can find one.

Offerings
- Bread
- Vegetables (except lettuce)
- Beer
- Wine
- Dark chocolate
- Brandy
- Scotch
- Apples
- Seeds
- Real plants
- Aquamarine
- Frankincense
- Colors: green, purple, brown, and black

Signs Osiris Is Calling You

Osiris will appear in your dreams if he wants to connect with you. He may not come himself, though. You may hear his name in your dreams or see his symbols.

The Experience of Connecting with Osiris

People who connected with Osiris felt that he was extremely focused and a little stern. However, he was good-natured, and he had a sense of humor.

Horus, the God of the Sky

Horus, god of the sky.
Jeff Dahl, CC BY-SA 4.0 <https://creativecommons.org/licenses/by-sa/4.0>, via Wikimedia Commons: https://commons.wikimedia.org/wiki/File:Horus_standing.svg

Hieroglyphic Name

Horus's name used to be spelled as ḥr.w, which meant falcon. It later came to be pronounced as ˈħaːruw then as ˈħaːrəʔ. The name went through different pronunciations over the years, and it was the ancient Greeks who called him Hōros, which is pronounced hôːros. The name is believed to have had other meanings in Latin, like "One who is above, over" or "the distant one," which obviously refers to his role as the god of the sky.

Worshiping Horus

Horus was worshiped all over Egypt, and there was a temple for him in Upper Egypt. Back in the day, ancient Egypt was split in two, and Horus was only worshiped in Southern Egypt. When the North and South were reunited, he was the Pharaoh of united Egypt. There are still, to this day, people who worship ancient Egyptian deities, including Horus. He was also worshiped in Greece. Several pagans still honor him and include him in their practices.

Symbols

- Falcon's head
- Eye of Horus
- Hawk
- Peacock

Correspondences

- The Sky
- War
- The sun
- The moon
- Protection

Myth

We mentioned in the last chapter how Horus became a king. However, there is more than one version of this story. Horus wasn't only concerned about the throne. He also wanted to avenge his father. He and Seth fought on more than one occasion. During one of these fights, Seth blinded Horus in his left eye. Thoth, the god of the moon and writing, healed him. His new eye was named wedjat, which became "The eye of Horus" and a symbol of protection. He became more adamant than ever about killing Seth, which he eventually did, and he finally avenged his father. After Seth's death, Horus became king.

Another story states that when the gods couldn't decide between Horus and Seth, instead of seeking Neith's help, Set and Horus were to undertake certain contests to determine which one of them was fit to be the king. In one of the contests, they turned into hippopotamuses and were supposed to go underwater to see who could stay there the longest. When underwater, Isis could have killed Seth, but she didn't. Horus was understandably angry with his mother, and he left to stay in the desert.

Seth found him, and this time he took out both of his eyes. However, Hathor, the goddess of fertility, healed him and made him whole again.

Eventually, the gods decided that Horus should be king since he won almost all the contests and proved himself worthy of the throne. Horus had shown courage, skill, honor, and determination in all versions.

Connecting with Horus

You can paint or draw the eye of Horus to connect with him and gain his protection. You can also create an altar and add statues and images of the deity and his eye. Wearing the Eye of Horus as an amulet may also help. Since he is the god of the sky, spend some time outdoors looking at the sky and thinking of Horus.

Offerings
- Bread
- Triangular cakes
- Iron
- Fresh red meat
- Incense
- Bread
- Cool water
- Candles
- Beer

Signs Horus Is Calling You

If Horus is calling you, he will appear in your dream, or you will see a hawk or a falcon in your dreams or real life. A friend may also give you an eye of Horus amulet as a gift.

The Experience of Connecting with Horus

When connecting with Horus, it is vital that you keep in mind that he is both a god and a king. So, treat him according to his rank and address him with respect. People who connect with him also feel he has become their guide and is always there with them as they constantly see falcons and Hawks. He also seems to be caring and protective.

Set the God of the Desert and Chaos

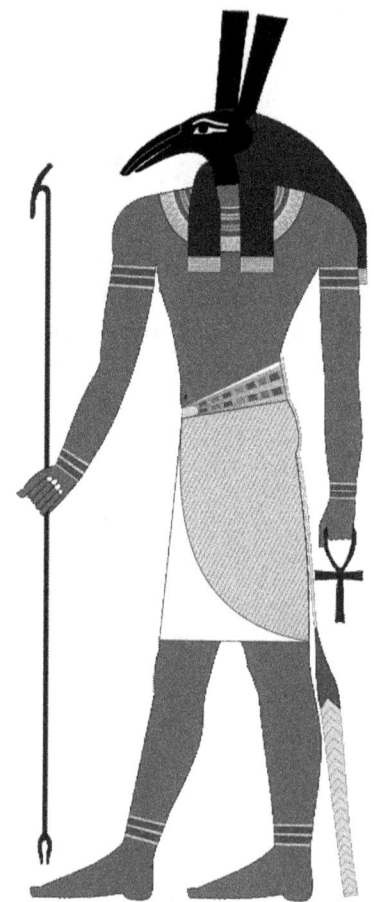

Set, god of the desert and chaos.
Jeff Dahl (talk · contribs), CC BY-SA 4.0 <https://creativecommons.org/licenses/by-sa/4.0>, via Wikimedia Commons: https://commons.wikimedia.org/wiki/File:Set.svg

Hieroglyphic Name

Set is the god Seth whom we have mentioned a few times in the book. The Greeks were the ones who gave him the name Seth. In Hieroglyphics, it was spelled as sth̬ and swth̬ and pronounced 'suw tix[j]. The meaning of the name remains a mystery.

Worshiping Set

Set was mainly worshiped in Upper Egypt. People found him admirable since he was strong and cunning. However, after he killed his brother, many of his followers began to regard him in a negative light.

Even the Greeks associated him with an evil force. Only in some areas of Egypt was he regarded as a chief deity. Set represents chaos and power, traits many people gravitate toward, which is why a few pagans still worship him.

Symbols
- Set animal
- Was Scepter

Correspondences
- Disorder
- Infertility
- Desert
- Storms
- Violence

Myth

We have mentioned Set a few times, and he appeared as the villain in all of them. He killed his brother and tried to kill his nephew. So, what drove Set to these actions? Set was always jealous of Osiris but what prompted him to murder his brother wasn't just his jealousy. His wife, Nephthys, transformed into Isis and slept with Osiris. They had a son Annubis, the god of the dead. When Set found out about this betrayal, he killed his brother. However, Set's anger was misplaced since Osiris thought she was his wife.

In one of the versions of the story where Horus became king, and Set was compensated by marrying two women, who were Ra's daughters, Ra offered Set a job. He would protect Ra's boat from the evil serpent Apep.

Connecting with Set

You can connect with Set by creating an altar or meditating. Some people connect with him by honoring him on his birthday. Get a red candle, carve his hieroglyphic name, and light it. Add to the altar any orange, yellow, or red items. Honoring Set on his birthday can help you develop a personal relationship with him.

Offerings
- Lettuce
- Red stones
- Cinnamon

- Handmade art
- Sandalwood
- Spicy food

Signs Set Is Calling You

You may see Set in your dreams if you sleep facing north. Someone may mention Set's name in your dream, or you may hear it on TV or see it online.

The Experience of Connecting with Set

People who connected with Set often compared him to the Norse god of chaos and mischief, Loki. For this reason, they always approach this prankster deity with caution. His followers don't find him evil. In fact, they find him a great god to work with.

Thoth the God of the Moon and Writing

Thoth, god of the moon and writing.
Jeff Dahl, CC BY-SA 4.0 <https://creativecommons.org/licenses/by-sa/4.0>, *via Wikimedia Commons:* https://commons.wikimedia.org/wiki/File:Thoth.svg

Hieroglyphic Name

Thoth's original name was Djehuty which is pronounced as *Je-hu-ti*. His name translates to "He who is like the Ibis," which is a type of bird that the god is depicted as. It is a common bird in Ancient Egypt and has come to be associated with wisdom. His name was written in various ways, like Jehuti, Tetu, Tahuti, and Tahuti. Thoth was often referred to as "Lord of divine words" and "Lord of Maat." It was the Greeks who referred to him as Thoth, which is the name commonly used.

Worshiping Thoth

Thoth was mainly worshiped in Upper Egypt, as his cult originated in a town called Khmunu. The Greeks referred to this town as Hermopolis, which is now called Al-Ashmūnayn. They associated Thoth with their god Hermes since both deities were considered messengers of the gods. The Greeks revered and highly admired him and considered him the source of all knowledge. There are still people around the world, including in America, who worship Thoth.

Symbols
- Ibis
- Scales
- Moon disk
- Baboon
- Papyrus scroll
- Writing palette
- Stylus
- Red pen

Correspondences
- Divine balance
- The moon
- Writing
- Learning
- Reckoning
- Wisdom
- Magic
- Healing
- Language

Myth

There is more than one story about Thoth's birth. One says that, like Ra, he also created himself. In another story, he was born from Ra's lips. In a different one, he was born from Set's forehead. We have mentioned that Thoth healed Horus's eye. However, Thoth was fair and didn't side with either of the conflicting deities. He also healed Set on multiple occasions. He wanted the contests between the gods to remain fair and refused to give one an advantage over another.

One of Ra's eyes, who was also his daughter, disagreed with him and decided to leave. Ra was unable to see when his eye disappeared and decided to send someone after her to bring her back. However, bringing her back wasn't going to be an easy task since she was so strong, and no one would be able to force her. This mission didn't only require someone who was physically strong but also smart and cunning.

In ancient Egyptian mythology, the goddess is often referred to as the distant goddess, and it was Thoth that Ra chose to bring her back. He disguised himself as a monkey and went after the goddess. In one version of the story, Thoth asked her to go back home about 1,077 times. He was cunning and persistent and didn't give up until he succeeded in his mission and brought her home. Ra was delighted by Thoth's success and awarded him the goddess Nehemtawy to be his consort.

Connecting with Thoth

To connect with Toth, research and learn as much as possible about him. Thoth admires learning, curiosity, and knowledge. You can also pray to him by setting up an altar and decorating it with ibis origami or statues.

Offerings

- Cool water
- Honey
- Orange juice
- Lemons
- Blackberries
- Apricots
- Chicken
- Tuna
- Salmon

- Lamb's ribs
- Onion
- Garlic
- Walnuts
- Quills
- Ibis feather
- Papyrus
- Pen
- Poetry

Signs Thoth Is Calling You

You may see the name Thoth everywhere. People may be posting stuff about him online, seeing his name in books, or hearing people talk about him. He or his symbols may also appear to you in your dreams. You may also feel connected to him or curious about him. Fulfill this curiosity and learn more about him because he loves curiosity.

The Experience of Connecting with Thoth

Some people call on Thoth when they experience writer's block or have an exam. According to them, the god is always happy to help, and since you will learn so much from him, they advise you to show gratitude and present offerings.

The gods of ancient Egypt have always been known for their wisdom. You can learn and grow once you begin working with them. Learn about the deities and choose the one who can help and guide you on your journey.

Chapter 5: Egyptian Symbols and Their Significance

Religion was a big part of ancient Egypt. Their gods played a huge role throughout their lives and even after death by helping them transition into the afterlife. The gods were always there to take care of mankind. For this reason, the physical and spiritual worlds were often intertwined with each other. This was clear from the presence of various symbols in their illustrations, objects, architecture, and amulets, especially the objects used by clergymen and the nobility. These symbols were very beneficial and practical for several reasons.

Like many other societies at the time, the ancient Egyptians were illiterate. Symbols provided a method for people from all walks of life to read hymns and poetry and communicate with one another. Symbols also had a magical significance and were used in various spells and rituals. This chapter will cover the most prominent Egyptian symbols and their significance.

The Ankh

Ankh symbol.
https://commons.wikimedia.org/wiki/File:Ankh-Symbol.svg

The Ankh is a very popular symbol. In fact, many people today wear it as jewelry or tattoo it over their bodies without realizing its meaning or knowing its origins. The Ankh looks like a cross with a looped top. It resembles a key, and it can grant its holder the secrets of existence. The Ankh is often referred to as "the key to life," and it symbolizes eternal life. The ring on the top of the Ankh represents the joining of man and woman, the heavens and the mortal world, and the journey between the two worlds.

This symbol was very powerful, which is why the Pharaohs and the gods were often depicted holding it. It is also associated with the Knot of Isis and her cult. When Isis grew more popular, more people became aware of the Ankh. The origin of the Ankh remains a mystery.

The Ankh in the Past

According to various ancient artworks and illustrations, the gods in the afterlife who judged the spirits of the dead usually had an Ankh in their hand. They would bring it to the deceased's nostrils so they could breathe in immortality. It was also used during purification ceremonies for the Pharaohs. Water by chains of Ankhs would be presented to him and poured over his head. This served as a reminder that the Pharaoh ruled under the gods and that they would return to him when he died.

The Ankh Today

Nowadays, people use the Ankh to bring prosperity, strength, and balance into their lives. Some Kemetic pagans use the Ankh as a symbol of their faith, and there are other worshippers from multiple faiths who see the Ankh as a symbol of life and wisdom. Isis followers use the ankh during their rituals as well.

The Djed Pillar

The Djed pillar is basically a column with a base that is broad, and it narrows as it rises. The top is easily recognized by its four parallel lines. The ancient Egyptians believed that these four lines represented the four corners of the planet. The number four was also heavily featured in ancient Egyptian mythology. They believed that it represented wholeness and completeness. The Djed pillar is often called "the Backbone of Osiris." It is associated with Osiris and symbolizes stability, strength, resurrection, and eternity. You can find this symbol in ancient Egyptian temples, amulets, and the book of the dead.

It is a symbol that is often connected to Isis and Osiris. It represented rebirth and resurrection, which was what Osiris experienced after Set murdered him. It acted as a fertility pole and was also linked to Osiris, who was the god of agriculture before becoming the god of the underworld. Osiris would flood the river Nile to fertilize the land.

The Djed Pillar in the Past

The ancient Egyptians used the Djed during their festivals. It acted as a fertility pole representing the balance between life and the afterlife. The Djed would be raised into the air to represent the rising crops, life rising from what once seemed dead, and the rising of a person's spirit from this realm to the next.

This symbol was also included on the bottom of coffins because it was associated with resurrection. The ancient Egyptians believed that it helped the deceased's soul stand and take its first steps toward the afterlife.

The Djed Pillar Today

You can include the Djedt in spells that will help bring balance and stability into your life.

The Eye of Horus/Wadjet

After Horus lost his left eye fighting with Set, Thoth restored it, and it was given the name Wadjet, and it protected Horus. For this reason, Wadjet became a symbol of healing and protection. It also represented good fortune, sacrifice, health, and royal power. The eye of Horus is one of ancient Egypt's most popular symbols.

The Eye of Horus in the Past

Wadjet was associated with magical abilities. The ancient Egyptians believed it was a powerful symbol with healing powers. For this reason, physicians at the time used it in their practices to measure the medicine ingredients. They also believed that it had immense mathematical knowledge.

The Eye of Horus Today

Nowadays, Wadject still represents similar themes as people associate it with protection, revelation, and wisdom. It is often compared to the eye of providence on the one-dollar bill. Some people associate it with control and manipulation since it resembles the symbol of the questionable group, the Illuminati. However, it is still regarded by many as a force for good. People use it to protect themselves against evil. They hang it in their homes as protection from physical and spiritual dangers. They also use it in various spells to attract positive energy and repel negative energy.

The Eye of Ra/The Udjat Eye

The eye of Ra is often linked to the Wadjet, as both were considered protective goddesses in ancient Egyptian mythology. The Udjat, as it was referred to, is often featured in various myths as the Distant Goddess we mentioned in the last chapter. There are different versions of this myth, but they all share one common theme, and that is the goddess ran away, and someone went after her to bring her back or trick her into coming back. The eye of Ra referred to either the Distant Goddess herself or those who were sent to bring her back.

The symbol also acted as Ra's, the creator's watchful eye over mankind – representing power, authority, peace, and rebirth.

The Eye of Ra in the Past

Just like its counterpart, the Udjat was used to repel negative energies and bring harmony. The ancient Egyptians also used it to protect themselves and their homes. They would paint it over their homes to bring good health, repel evil spirits, and break harmful spells. Fishermen also painted it on their boats before they went fishing to protect themselves and their boats from evil spirits. The Eye of Ra was often used to protect the dead when they traveled to the next world.

The Eye of Ra Today

The eye of Ra is as popular today as it was thousands of years ago. It is used in Reiki to symbolize knowledge and enlightenment. People associate it with the Third Eye, which connects us to our truest selves. You can also wear it to protect yourself from the "evil eye" or people who wish you harm.

The Scarab

The scarab is a beetle that was extremely popular in ancient Egypt until the arrival of Christianity. You can find this symbol in artwork and illustrations. The scarab beetle is a type of dung beetle. The beetle would roll animal droppings into a ball and use them as breeding chambers for their eggs as it provided food for the young when the eggs hatched. When the ancient Egyptians saw this process, they associated the beetle with the gods since its lifecycle represented resurrection, creation of life, and transformation. The scarab was also associated with Khepri, the god of the morning sun, who had a face like a scarab beetle.

The Scarab in the Past

The letter of the scarab in hieroglyphics is linked to growth and transformation. For this reason, the ancient Egyptian used the scarab symbol to describe the ranks of officers in the government.

The Scarab Today

The ancient Egyptians associated the scarab with good luck. You can wear it as an amulet to bring good fortune into your life.

The Ka

The ka symbol means soul or spirit. Its hieroglyphic symbol is shoulders and arms bent and pointing upward at the elbow. It is associated with the new soul of an infant who is resurrected after death. Simply put, it was the essence of a person, and it had a huge impact on all areas of one's life. The gods were the ones to bestow ka among mankind since they were the ones that gave them life or the spirit. The ka of a royal was different from that of the people. The ka of royals was regarded as original or unique, while the soul of a regular person was of lesser value and belonged to the gods.

The Ka in the Past

The ancient Egyptians considered the ka a symbol of protection and acted as a guardian. It was responsible for making a person kind, compassionate, and honorable.

The Ka Today

People use the ka symbol because they believe it can put them on the right path in life.

The Ouroboros

The Ouroboros is one of the oldest Egyptian signs. It is probably as old as the creation of the universe. It was created when Ra willed himself into existence. When he first appeared, he took the form of a serpent which is why the Ouroboros symbol is a serpent eating its own tail. The symbol represents Ra's journeys and is associated with recreation and rebirth. The Ouroboros symbolizes the circle of life, time, death, fertility, and good luck.

The Ouroboros in the Past

Ouroboros was engraved in the tomb of Tutankhamen because it represented life after death. The symbol was a part of Norse and Greek mythology as well.

The Ouroboros Today

The Ouroboros is depicted as either a serpent or a dragon forming a circle and eating its own tail. It is usually associated with alchemy.

The Uraeus

A cobra represents the goddess of royalty, Wadjet, representing the authority of the divine, royalty, and sovereignty. According to ancient Egyptian mythology, the Uraeus symbolizes protection and has magical powers. In hieroglyphics, it was associated with a shrine.

The Uraeus in the Past

The Uraeus acted as a royal symbol to prove that the Pharaoh on the throne was the legitimate king. For that reason, kings are often depicted wearing the Uraeus symbol to prove their legitimacy. The goddess Wadjet offered protection to the Pharaoh wearing this symbol.

The Uraeus Today

People include the Uraeus in their rituals because it has magical powers. You can also wear it for protection.

The Was Scepter

The Was scepter is a staff with an animal head, often a canine, and a fork at the end. This symbol was heavily influenced by the Hekat scepter, which represented royal power. In ancient Egyptian legends, the color of the staff and the fork often changed depending on who was holding it. They believed that the sky was built on four Was scepters. The ancient Egyptians referred to it as the "sculptor of the earth." It represented completeness. Each god and goddess had their own scepters like Isis and Ra, and their concept changed according to the god who was holding it. For instance, when Isis held it, it became associated with fertility. When Ra held it, it represented rebirth, and when Horus held it, it was associated with the sky.

The Was Scepter in the Past

The ancient Egyptians used the Was scepter with the ankh and the Djed, as is clear from their illustrations. When combined together, these three symbols provide long life, strength, and success.

The Was Scepter Today

Some people use the Was scepter in magic rituals.

The Crook and Flail

The crook and flail represent the power of a king. They were symbols of the god Osiris and his rule over Egypt. These symbols are also related to Horus and his myth. When he defeated Set and took his place on the throne, he took Osiris's crook and flail to prove that he was the legitimate king.

The Crook and Flail in the Past

Before they became sacred symbols, the shepherds used the crook with their goats and harvested certain plants with the flail. Osiris became associated with these symbols because he was the god of agriculture. In addition to being symbols of a legitimate and powerful king, the crook and flail became reminders of the past and old traditions as well.

The Shen

The Shen is depicted as a circle made of a rope. The circle doesn't have a beginning or an end to illustrate wholeness and completeness. It is a symbol of infinity, eternity, divine protection, and an unbroken bond. The word "*shen*" means "encircle." This symbol is quite similar to the Greek omega symbol, which also represents infinity. In various illustrations, we can see gods and goddesses holding the Shen. Isis and Horus were often depicted holding one. As a result, ancient Egyptians held the symbol in high regard and considered it a symbol of perfection.

The Shen in the Past

Shen amulets were very popular in ancient Egypt. All Egyptians, from slaves to farmers to kings, wore one. They also engraved it on tombs and temples.

The Shen Today

If you are looking to feel whole or complete, you can wear this symbol of wholeness and completeness.

The Sesen

The Sesen symbol is a lotus flower often associated with ancient Egypt, representing life, creation, rebirth, and the sun. It was often compared to the sun because at night, the lotus flower closes and goes underwater, and, just like the sun, it emerges the next day. The life of the lotus represents very important themes like rebirth. It is also associated with Ra, who willed himself into existence by emerging from the water "nun." It is a symbol of rebirth, regeneration, enlightenment, and purity.

The Sensen in the Past

The lotus flower played a huge role in ancient Egyptian art as it was painted or engraved on amulets, shrines, and temples. It was also a symbol of Upper Egypt. This symbol was popular among the cult of Osiris, the god of the underworld. Its disappearance at night and emergence in the morning were linked to themes of death and resurrection.

The Lotus Today

The lotus flower is the main ingredient in many spells. The symbol itself can be used in various rituals that are associated with purity, cleanliness, or rebirth.

The Ben-Ben

Although you may be unfamiliar with the name ben-ben, you will most definitely recognize the symbol. The ben-ben are the pyramids of Egypt. Nothing is more associated with the country and its history than these famous monuments. The place where the pyramids stand is where creation began, as Ra stood there before he created mankind. The pyramids stand on the ground and rise toward the heavens. In one of the myths about creation, there was only darkness and chaos before the world came into existence. The pyramids or ben-ben were the first dry land created where Ra stood and began creating the world. For this reason, the pyramids were associated with creation.

The Ben-Ben in the Past

Ancient Egyptians wore the Ben-Ben symbol as an amulet, and they were crafted as statues and engraved on tombs and temples.

The Ben-Ben Today

The pyramids have always been mysterious and enchanting. There are people who believe that they have magical powers. As a result of their triangular shape, they can be used in healing rituals like healing the seven chakras.

The Feather of Maat

As mentioned in a previous chapter, Maat was either the goddess of justice or justice itself. She weighed the heart of the deceased against the feather of Maat to determine if they were good individuals who lived their lives in the service of others or led selfish lives. The feather of Matt is one of the most prominent symbols in ancient Egypt as it determines how people will spend their afterlife. Without the feather, it would be impossible to weigh the hearts, and thus the dead would have no place to go. Simply put, the feather of Maat was the foundation of the afterlife. Maat was associated with justice, order, harmony, balance, and truth.

The Feather of Maat in the Past

When the deceased reach the afterlife, they must stand in front of Osiris, where they will be judged by their heart being placed on a scale and weighed against a feather. If the heart's weight was lighter than the feather, it meant that they achieved good deeds when they were alive and deserved to spend eternity in the land of the field of the reeds, the equivalent to heaven or a good place. However, if the heart was heavier than the feather, they didn't lead a good or selfless life and would be devoured by the goddess Ammit, and they would cease to exist.

The Feather of Maat Today

The feather of Maat was a white ostrich feather. People who want to connect with Maat use an ostrich feather or any white feather when meditating to help them reach out to the goddess.

Ancient Egypt is filled with many secrets and mysteries. Their symbols are fascinating. Each one has a story behind it and can be used in various rituals and spells to this day. All these symbols can also be used to help you connect with your favorite deity. Since each god and goddess has their own symbols, you can learn about them and their myths and use them in meditation, decorate the deity's altar, tattoo them onto your body, or wear them as jewelry to keep the gods close to your heart.

Chapter 6: Egyptian Amulets and How to Make Them

Ancient Egyptian symbols held magical power. They were so powerful that they were also used as magical symbols in other belief systems and hermetic orders like the Rosicrucians.

These symbols don't simply have magical powers when written down. You can also create three-dimensional amulets of these symbols to aid you in your magical and religious practices.

If you're wondering how to create ancient Egyptian amulets, you're in the right place. In this chapter, you will explore the idea of ancient Egyptian amulets in greater detail, so you can understand why the Egyptians prized them. This chapter will also offer a few techniques to create your own amulets, which you can use in your spiritual and magical practice.

Understanding Ancient Egyptian Amulets

Ancient Egyptians used amulets for numerous reasons, and based on archaeological discoveries, the use of amulets was ubiquitous in Ancient Egypt. They were used for protection, in regeneration magic, as part of funerary rites, and much more.

Amulets were never far removed from ancient Egyptian magic. Even the most non-magical seeming of these amulets involved a level of magical practice from the amulet user. The amulet needed to be "activated," and this could only be done when the user recited a spell over the amulet.

These spells were often recorded in papyrus, many of which have survived and give us a better understanding of how ancient Egyptians used amulets in their daily lives.

Excavations in Egypt occur almost year-round, and much of what is found is either fragmented or intact amulets. Given the sheer volume of amulets available for scholars and people interested in ancient Egypt and ancient Egyptian magic, most people now categorize amulets as belonging to one of six distinct groupings or types of amulets.

These groupings are:

Amulets of Deities and Sacred Animals

This is a relatively self-evident classification of amulets.

The ancient Egyptian pantheon features over 1000 deities, many (if not all) of which also have a sacred form. Not all of them were represented in amulet form – amulets were used to ask the represented deity for protection or to use their powers to help you achieve your goals.

Amulets in this category we're sometimes elaborate and include the entire figure of the deity being invoked. However, these amulets were often relatively expensive and not accessible to everyone. The solution was to create amulets displaying their sacred animals.

A deity's sacred animal is a representation of themselves as gods. It was believed that if amulets were created in the shape of a given deity's sacred animal or other symbols, that deity would know that you were actually invoking them rather than the animal.

However, the challenge for archaeologists is that determining who each amulet was meant to invoke could often be difficult. There were only so many ancient animals to go around in Ancient Egypt and far too many deities.

Popular amulets like lioness head amulets remain a mystery for scholars. After all, a lioness head amulet could represent Sekhmet. It could also represent other deities, such as Bastet, Tefnut, and even the male deity, Wadjet. The only way to distinguish who a given amulet was meant for was based on engravings and context clues.

Amulets of Protection

Again, the name is relatively self-explanatory. These amulets were meant to shield the bearer from bad luck, providing them with good luck and protecting their life. The scarab is the most popular version of an amulet for protection, and the next section will go into the critical role the scarab played in Egyptian religious life.

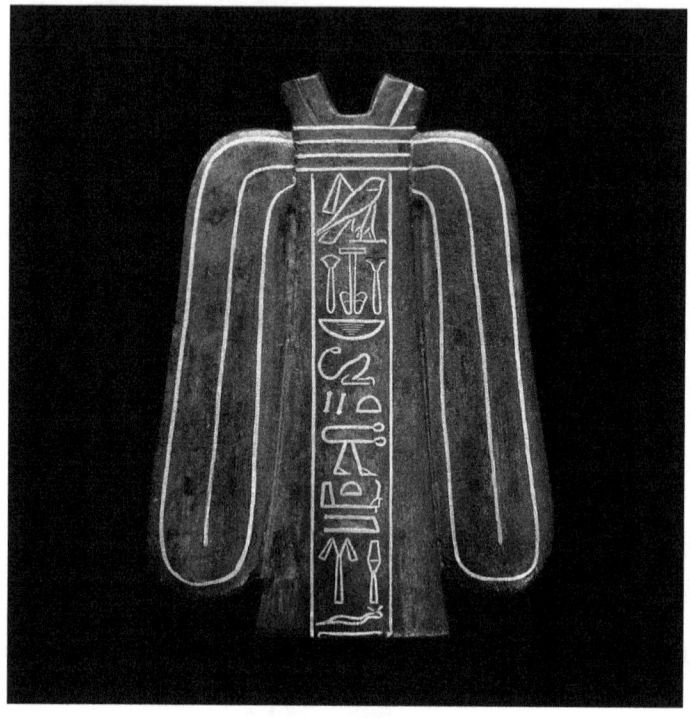

Knot of Isis.
Rama, CC BY-SA 3.0 FR <https://creativecommons.org/licenses/by-sa/3.0/fr/deed.en>, via Wikimedia Commons: https://commons.wikimedia.org/wiki/File:Isis_knot-E_4358-IMG_9355-black.JPG

A unique protection amulet was the Tyet of Isis. Also known as the *knot* (or girdle of Isis), this symbol was linked to the goddess Isis. It looks a lot like an Ankh, but the arms on the side are curved downward instead of sticking straight out. It symbolizes similar things to the Ankh, translating to life and wellbeing. The shape also resembles a knot of cloth. Some suggest that it is a representation of a bandage used to absorb menstrual blood. This amulet was used to protect the dead, and one of the first Tyet amulets was found in a tomb from the First Dynasty.

Scarab Amulets for the Living

Scarabs were an enormously popular type of amulet among the ancient Egyptians, and this popularity continued from the Middle Kingdom through the pharaonic period and beyond. Not only were they used as amulets, but the shape of the scarab was also used as part of both administrative and personal seals and decorative jewelry.

Scarabs were considered a representation of the deity Khepri, who represents the rising sun, creation, and the renewal of life. He was considered an aspect of the sun deity Ra and represented the morning sun (Ra was the midday sun and Atum the evening sun).

Additionally, ancient Egyptians viewed the scarab beetle as a magical creature. This stemmed from a misunderstanding of the beetle's life cycle – adult scarabs lay their eggs in dung balls that are buried underground. To unknowing observers, the hatching of young scarab beetles can be mistaken for them emerging fully formed out of dung, an unlikely and magical event of self-creation. For this reason, the Egyptian term for scarab literally translates to "to come into being."

Furthermore, as part of gathering dung balls in which to lay their eggs, the scarabs roll these balls across the landscape. Egyptians saw this act as similar to the sun's movement from the east to the west.

These two factors caused the young sun god – Khepri – to become undeniably linked to Ancient Egyptian religion. Khepri was a scarab-headed god, and he was thought to be reborn every morning at sunrise in the form of a winged scarab beetle.

Because of the scarab's ability to regenerate and rejuvenate and its links to the sun god, scarab amulets were used as protective amulets for the living. Commemorative scarabs were made by pharaohs and used to commemorate military victories or sent out as diplomatic gifts, and others were found with inscriptions of royal names. Scarabs with royal names inscribed were often created during a pharaoh's rule – the more scarabs with his name found, the longer (and better) he ruled.

Lots of scarabs have been found, and many of those were inscribed with the name of King Tuthmosis III. Many of these date to after his reign – these were likely created due to his worship. All pharaohs were worshiped as gods after death, but popular worship of Tuthmosis III seems to have continued centuries after his relatively rare death. This case was repeated (though in fewer numbers) in the case of Rameses II, Rameses the Great, who is regarded as perhaps the greatest Egyptian Pharaoh (along with the aforementioned Tuthmosis III).

Amulets of Assimilation

Amulets of assimilation are likely to have been the oldest form of amulets. The oldest ones were not physical representations of Egyptian symbols – rather, they were representations of parts of a human or animal body.

These amulets were believed to give the bearer the power represented by the body part.

One of the most important amulets of assimilation was the heart amulet, created to resemble a human heart. Ancient Egyptians believed the heart was the most important of all human organs, and they considered it to be the seat of intelligence – the place from where our feelings, actions, thoughts, and memories originated.

These amulets were placed on the upper torso of every Egyptian mummy – they served as almost a "replacement," ensuring the mummy would have a heart should its mummified heart be destroyed. The heart was the only organ that was left within the body during mummification, as its importance meant that the deceased would require it in the afterlife.

Heart amulets also served as a way to protect a mummy's heart and to ensure that the deceased would be positively received during the Weighing of the Heart.

Amulets of Power

These were amulets that conferred power upon the bearer or represented the bearer's power. These most commonly took the form of royal symbols, such as:

- The red crown
- Uraeus serpent
- Djed pillar

Over time, these amulets were no longer limited to use by royals and those to whom royalty gave the amulets. They were common in ancient Egyptian burials, and many scholars believe they represent the greater access to mummification – where it was once limited to royalty. Over time, it became accessible to everyone.

Other amulets of power included symbols that had innate powers. Bearers believed that using these amulets would transfer the power of the object to them. Amulets of power were representations of generally inanimate objects.

Amulets of Possessions, Offerings, and Property

As the name implies, these amulets were replicas of a person's property and possessions and any offerings they made to the deities or the deceased.

Amulets of property and possessions represented items that would be needed by the deceased in the afterlife and ranged from eating vessels, writing tablets, clothes, beauty materials, and more. These items were also generally present in a person's tomb. However, if grave robbers stole them, the belief was that the amulets would magically transform into the real items, ensuring that the deceased would experience no difficulties in the afterlife.

Amulets of offerings generally took the form of replicas of food offerings. Food offerings were placed outside ancient Egyptian tombs, similar to how we leave offerings on a person's grave today. The belief was that these offerings would be the food and drink that would sustain a person in the afterlife. Occasionally, offerings included other objects, including weapons, combs, and hairpins – anything the deceased's family thought would be useful or desirable in the afterlife.

However, it was the food offerings that were the most important. Because of this, amulets of food offerings were placed in the tomb at the burial. If the deceased's descendants did not present other food offerings, like the amulets of property and possessions, they would magically take on the form of the real item, ensuring the person remained nourished in the afterlife.

One unique amulet in this category was the situla amulet. "Situla" is the Latin word for "bucket" or "pail" and refers to a series of bucket-shaped vessels found in multiple cultures. It was used as part of the daily ceremony in which the deceased was offered food and drink offerings, and, in this case, the situla would have contained water or milk.

However, it was also used in magical rituals, and the situla used during these rituals was believed to contain a liquid with healing properties. Situla amulets were placed on the throats of the deceased, and they were believed to have the same healing powers as the liquid they contained when used in rituals.

Making Your Own Egyptian Amulets

While it is possible to buy pre-made Egyptian amulets, many people prefer to hand-make their magical tools where possible. If this is the case, it is possible for you to make your own Egyptian amulets.

These amulets can be made from various materials, including metal, wood, and faience. The material you choose depends on what you're most comfortable working with. However, out of all the options, the most convenient (and easiest) to use is quick-drying polymer clay.

The first step is to choose a design for your amulet. You'll need to choose an amulet type and symbol that matches what you'll use it for. For example, if you're looking for an amulet of protection, a scarab or Tyet knot are popular choices. Similarly, you might choose a wedjat eye amulet if you are looking for an amulet to help with healing and recovery.

Once you know the shape of the amulet you want, you can move on to actually making your amulet. Here's what you need to do:

1. Clean a space you can use as a work area.
2. Place scrap paper over the surface on which you will be working. This will protect the surface from any damage while you make your amulet.
3. Roll out your clay until you get the desired thickness. You can use your hand for this step.
4. Sketch the amulet shape onto the clay. If you're good at drawing, you could do this freehand. However, if you're not the greatest artist, you can print out the amulet's design using an inkjet printer with ink meant to bleed when wet. Then, lay the freshly printed image face down on the clay so that the ink is in contact with the clay, and rub the paper to transfer the image to the clay. The print should be in contact with the clay for 30 seconds to 1 minute. When you feel it has transferred, peel a small corner of the paper to see if your guess is right. If it has transferred, you can peel away the full print. If not, let it stay for a few more seconds. Ideally, you should do this with fresh clay, as it will be moist. However, if you do not have access to fresh clay, you can use water to dampen the back of the image when you're rubbing the paper.
5. Once the design is on the clay, cut it out using a modeling tool. Remove the excess clay and store it away, leaving the amulet to air dry. If the clay you're using isn't an air-drying one, bake it for a few seconds in your oven.
6. If you want, paint your amulet with acrylic paint, watercolors, or oil paint.
7. Once the amulet is dry, punch a hole in it and run a string through it if you want to wear it as a necklace, bracelet, or another type of jewelry.

Alternatively, if you're confident in your artistic skills, you could simply sculpt the amulet of your choice with clay and reference images.

Keep in mind that making your own amulets is not a necessity. If you need a more complex design and aren't confident of your artistic abilities, you need a freestanding amulet, and you aren't a sculptor, or you simply don't have the time to make your own can always buy a pre-made amulet. Remember, most ancient Egyptians would have bought their amulets rather than crafting them with their hands. Your amulets won't lose power for having been bought rather than handmade.

How to Cleanse Your Amulet

Cleansing your amulet is a relatively easy process. All you need to do is wash it in a saltwater bath and then pass it through incense smoke. While you do so, visualize all the energies that the amulet or the base materials you used may have accumulated before it reached your hands and took its current shape. Visualize these energies leaving the amulet, disappearing into the universe around you, sinking into the saltwater, or sinking into the ground.

Your amulet is now pure. If you visualize the energies passing into the saltwater, dispose of the saltwater. If not, you can release it into the ocean or the nearest body of water.

How to Set Your Intentions into Your Amulet

In general, you don't need to set intentions into Egyptian amulets. Unlike many modern designs, each Egyptian amulet has its own purpose.

However, there may be occasions when you want to direct the power of your amulet for a specific purpose. You should plan your goal first; then, write it down on a piece of paper, parchment, or papyrus.

Once this is ready, prepare your altar and have a quick ritual bath. Then, you should:

1. Cleanse the space of negative energy and make a circle around your altar.
2. Pray to the deities and call the elements while lighting your altar candles.
3. Cleanse the talisman as described above.
4. Dress your spell candle.
5. Read your goal while lighting your spell candle. This will serve as your magical incantation.
6. Hold the talisman in your hands and repeat the incantation several times, visualizing your goal and visualizing its energy pouring into

the talisman.
7. Pray to the deity of your choice, asking them for their help.
8. Meditate on your goal.
9. Place the talisman where it will be kept, or wear it if you will be wearing it on your person.
10. Thank the deity. This can involve an offering - it's up to you.
11. Close the circle.

Amulets are not the only ancient Egyptian magical tools you can create. If you want to know about more ancient Egyptian magical tools that you can incorporate into your practice, turn the page and keep reading. In the next chapter, we'll cover tools like the ushabti, sistrum, shendyt, and magic wand to help you understand their history and how you can create them at home (or otherwise find them). We'll also explore how you can make an altar to the deity of your choice.

Chapter 7: More Magical Tools to Create

As mentioned in the previous chapter, amulets are not the only ancient Egyptian magical tools you can access and use today. The ancient Egyptians used several tools and objects considered to be magical or powerful in their own right, and many of these are accessible and usable today.

In this chapter, we'll examine some of these tools. We'll cover their history and look at ways you can access the tools and use them in your magical practice today. We'll also look at ways in which you can create a shrine or altar to a particular Egyptian deity (or deities), so you have a space in your home where you can worship them.

Book of the Dead

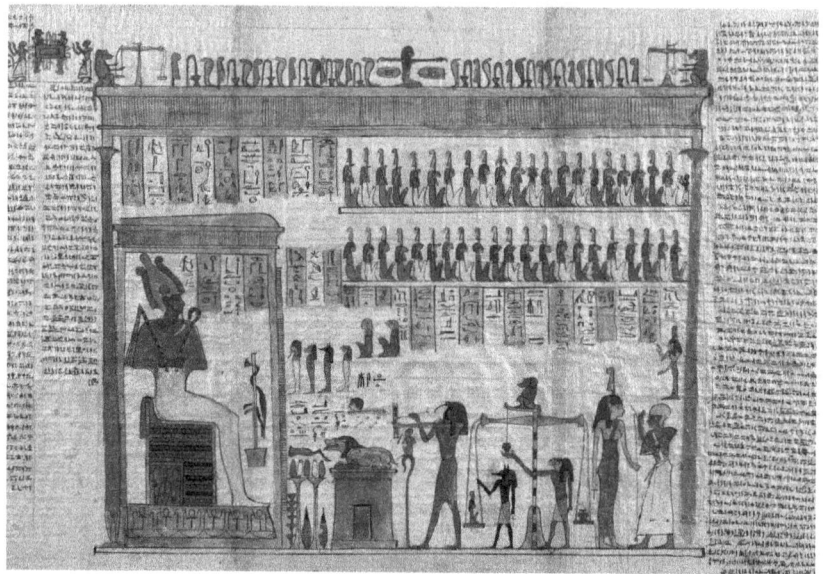

The Book of the Dead.
https://commons.wikimedia.org/wiki/File:Book_of_the_dead_egypt.jpg

Perhaps the best-known ancient Egyptian magical tool today is the Book of the Dead. This book wasn't a single canonical book that was replicated. Rather, it is the common name for a collection of funerary texts with spells and magical formulas that were placed in the tomb.

This text was believed to protect the deceased and help them through their journey to the underworld (the Duat). We know of at least 192 spells that were included in the Book of the Dead. There was no single text that contained all the known spells, and they have been collected from different extant examples of the Book of the Dead.

Each spell has a different purpose. For example, some are meant to provide the deceased with mystical knowledge in the afterlife, while others are meant to help with the preservation of different aspects of the deceased's body and personality. Even others are meant to protect the deceased person from forces hostile to them as they make their way through the underworld.

A Book of the Dead was an expensive item. It was produced by scribes, and the cost of a copy could be as much as half of the yearly pay of a laborer. Because of this, copies were generally found in the tombs of the elite, including royalty, officials, scribes, and priests.

How to Make Your own Book of the Dead

The Book of the Dead is one of the ancient Egyptian magical tools that should be bought rather than created. Unless you're skilled at writing hieroglyphics, copying it down is a complicated task, and there's a strong possibility that you will make mistakes.

However, if you are skilled at hieroglyphics, copies of the Book of the Dead are available online, and you can use them as a source to create your own reproduction. The production process is a relatively simple undertaking beyond having knowledge of the symbols. All you need to do is copy them on paper or parchment.

You can use the Book of the Dead as part of your own death and mourning rituals. It can be placed in the grave with a deceased loved one to protect them on their journey to the afterlife or as part of the offerings you leave for them on your altar. You can even leave it as an offering on a loved one's grave or place of burial.

Sekhem Scepter

A sekhem was a ritual scepter used to symbolize power and might. The word "sekhem" was often incorporated into a royal's name, such as Sekhemkhet, a pharaoh from the Old Kingdom.

Royalty and other important officials used it. It was also considered to be a symbol of underworld deities, especially Anubis. It was a sacred object of Anubis's, and the god was frequently shown in a reclining position with the sekhem positioned behind him.

Because of its connection to Anubis, the sekhem was also used during ceremonial offerings to the dead. It was held by the person making an offering in the right hand. Next, it was waved over any offerings to be made, as ritual spells were being cast before the offerings were presented.

The shape of the sekhem had some variations but generally resembled the flat head of a paddle over a long handle.

How to Make Your Own Sekhem

Sekhem scepters can be hard to find online. If you're not very good with your hands, you can get a custom-made one. Alternatively, you can start with a wood flat-headed paddle and carve it down to resemble a scepter.

You can even carve your own from scratch if you are skilled at wood carving.

If none of these options is possible, you can create your own symbolic sekhem. You don't need carving skills for this - simply a block of wood, some paper, and tools to cut wood.

Draw the design of a sekhem on your piece of paper, or trace it from a design you find online. Transfer the design to the block of wood. Then, cut out the shape of the sekhem. You don't need to do much, unlike carving an actual sekhem or cutting a paddle down to shape. While this sekhem will not be perfect, it will be enough.

You can use your sekhem when creating altars for the deceased. Use it when making offerings to loved ones who have passed away, and wave it over an offering as the ancient Egyptians would have done. You should wave it four or five times for each offering.

Crook and Flail

Crook and flail.
Jeff Dahl, CC BY-SA 4.0 <https://creativecommons.org/licenses/by-sa/4.0>, via Wikimedia Commons: https://commons.wikimedia.org/wiki/File:Crook_and_flail.svg

The crook and flail were symbols of royal power in ancient Egypt and were only used by the pharaoh and, in exceedingly rare cases, by other high officials and priests. They held a lot of power and represented the power of the Pharaoh. They were never depicted with the gods.

The only deity that was an exception to this rule was Osiris, as the crook and the flail were originally his symbols that would develop into important signifiers of the pharaoh's rule. The crook was a shepherd's crook and looked similar to a cane with a hooked handle. The flail had three strands of beads attached to a stiff rod. The strands could vary in size, design, and complexity.

How to Make Your Own Crook and Flail

Due to their ubiquity as items carried by pharaohs, the crook and flail are easily purchasable in prop form. However, if you cannot find one in your local store or you prefer to make your own, the process is very simple.

All you'll need is some Christmas ornaments, super glue, and paint (gold and blue).

1. Take a large plastic ornament candy cane and spray-paint it gold.
2. Once the paint dries, snap it in half.
3. Paint blue stripes on each half so that the cane alternates between blue and gold stripes.
4. Allow the halves to dry.
5. Put the half with the candy cane head aside. This is your crook.
6. Take three plastic ornament icicles and spray-paint them gold.
7. Allow them to dry, and paint blue stripes as you did with the candy cane.
8. Once the paint dries, use the loop of string attached to them to tie them to the "flail" half of the candy cane. Use super glue to hold them in place.
9. Let the super glue dry.
10. Your crook and flail are ready.

You can use your crook and flail as offerings to Osiris or on an altar to the deity when praying to him.

Ushabti Figure

Also known as a shabti, an ushabti figure was a type of small statuette found in Egyptian tombs. Ushabtis were placed in large numbers in graves – the higher the person's status in life, the more ushabti figures they had in their tombs.

These figures were meant to serve as servants and laborers for the deceased in the afterlife, conducting manual tasks on their behalf. Because of this, many of these figurines generally carried farming implements.

How to Make Your Own Ushabti Figure

An ushabti figure is a relatively easy magical tool to make. Almost any human-form figurine can stand in for an ushabti. If you don't already have human-like figurines at home, one easy way to get some is to buy children's dolls.

If you want to make them a bit more formal, you can use the figurine as a starting-off point and then sew clothes for it. This allows you to personalize the figurine by creating different clothes for each figure.

Alternatively, you can also make your ushabti figures out of wood, clay, stone, enamel, faience, metal, glass, or terracotta. You can use any material you're comfortable with – in fact, the earliest ushabtis were made from wax. They were generally made to resemble mummies, so you can also use scrap cloth and draw a human figure.

Like other ancient Egyptian magical grave goods, ushabti figures can be used in altars for the deceased. They can be offered in ways similar to how the ancient Egyptians offered them, as magical figurines that reduced the physical labor expected of the deceased in the afterlife.

Nemes

The nemes was a striped headdress or head cloth used by the pharaohs as a symbol of their power. Though it isn't a crown, its use was limited to pharaohs and Roman emperors. If you've ever seen an image of the mask of Tutankhamun, the nemes is the striped headdress depicted on the mask.

The use of this piece of cloth has evolved over the years. The members of the Hermetic Order of the Golden Dawn used the nemes as part of their ritualistic clothes.

How to Make Your Own Nemes

You can easily find a pattern for a nemes online. Make it out of white or yellow cloth, and paint the stripes with blue paint.

You can use your nemes as ceremonial garb when conducting your rituals. The nemes were also worn by statues of the deities Osiris, Isis, and Nephthys. It can be used to decorate your altars dedicated to these deities.

Sistrum

The sistrum is a musical instrument that was used in dances and religious ceremonies and was often seen with Hathor and Ihy (her son). The handle was modeled after a cow's head, taking up a u-shape that looked like the head and horns. Hathor was generally depicted as a goddess wearing a cow headdress or as a reclining cow, which linked her to the sistrum.

The instrument was used during the flooding of the Nile. It was shaken over the waters of the Nile as a way to frighten Set, the god of disorder and storms. It was also linked to the goddesses Amun, Horus, Bat, Bast, and Isis. It is still used in rituals of the Oriental Orthodox Churches.

How to Make Your Own Sistrum

You can either buy a model of a sistrum or make your own model from clay.

The sistrum can be used to decorate altars to the deities Isis, Amun, Horus, Hathor, Bat, and Bast. You can also use it while performing fertility and weather magic, especially magic associated with rain.

Birth Tusk/Magic Wand

The birth tusk is a magic wand used by the ancient Egyptians when performing protective magic. These wands were originally made with hippopotamus ivory, hence their name. They were occasionally made of wood.

However, hippopotamus ivory was the most common material. This is because the fearsome hippopotamus was thought to help ward off evil. It was used to protect against illnesses and evil spirits and was commonly carried by nurses during childbirth as a way to protect the mother and child.

How to Make Your Own Birth Tusk

You can carve your own birth tusk out of wood. To infuse it with the power of the hippopotamus, carve it with a hippopotamus symbol. It should also be carved with other protective symbols.

The birth tusk/magic wand can be used when performing fertility and protective magic. It can be used in place of your existing wand or in concert with it. You can also use it when performing childbirth rituals as a protective tool.

Shendyt

The shendyt was an Egyptian garment similar to a skirt or a kilt. Men wore it around the waist and reached just above the knees. While commoners usually wore it, it was also worn by officials, royalty, and even pharaohs. Additionally, it was worn by male deities in statutory and artistic representations.

How to Make Your Own Shendyt

You can easily find a pattern for a shendyt online. You can make it out of scrap cloth – linen was the most common fabric used in ancient Egypt, though you can use any other material you have on hand.

You can wear the shendyt when performing ceremonies and rituals.

How to Make an Egyptian Altar

The ancient Egyptians made offerings to the deities on altars located outside the main sanctuary of a temple dedicated to that deity. They were also placed in royal courts and in the homes of worshippers.

To make your own altar, you will need the following:

- Representations of the four elements
- Offerings to the deity to whom you are making an altar
- A focal point – a symbol of the deity would be a good option
- The magical tools you will be using
- Egyptian symbols and amulets

To make the altar, you will need a table or any other flat surface. Place each representation of the elements on each of the corners of the table.

Cover the table with a cloth decorated with ancient Egyptian symbols. You can paint these on or transfer them to the cloth with stickers.

Once your altar is dressed, place your focal point in the center of the altar, and place the amulets around the altar. Start an offering ritual, and place your offerings on the altar to the deity.

You can use this altar to worship the deity, perform your regular rituals, or use it in concert with any other altars you have set up. People often set up at least two rituals – one dedicated to the deity of their choice and the other to the ancestors and the deceased.

Magical tools can also be used in other ways, such as when performing divination magic and plant magic. This book will explain how to perform ancient Egyptian divination and plant magic. The next chapter will cover divination magic in detail, while the chapter after that will explore sacred plant and herb magic.

We'll also explore spells and rituals you can perform using your magical tools. This will include spells and rituals for a variety of purposes, including protection magic, healing magic, and love magic. Later in this book, you'll find step-by-step instructions on performing each ritual from start to finish.

By the end, you'll know how to use all your tools and amulets to their fullest extent. You'll have a better understanding of ancient Egyptian magic and be ready to incorporate it into your regular rituals and magic practice.

Chapter 8: Methods of Divination

The most well-documented method of divination in ancient Egypt was scrying, although there are records of several other techniques used around that time. Oil scrying, moon divination, and dream interpretation are just some of the most common methods ancient Egyptians used to reveal fate. This chapter discusses these techniques and how divination was perceived in ancient Egypt. You'll also be provided with several techniques you, as a contemporary practitioner, can incorporate into your divinatory practices. To help you get the most out of any technique, it's recommended that you also use grounding, cleansing, and protection rituals as part of your preparation process.

Divination in Ancient Egypt

Unlike in modern practices (where divination is often used for self-exploration), in ancient Egypt, the primary focus of divinatory practices was to find answers about present situations. Practitioners would try to obtain all the valuable information they could get about the present. They would then use this information to change their behavior, which, in turn, had the power to change future outcomes. In more challenging situations, they would ask a deity for answers and guidance, compelling them to help the practitioners make the desired changes.

Some of the ways the art of divination was used in ancient Egypt (and can still be used) was to find answers, and items, reconnect with people, and predict the future using dreams, omens, and visions. That is to predict possible outcomes of future events and situations, not exactly how things will happen. Even ancient Egyptians knew divination couldn't give a practitioner direct answers. It would only guide them toward the most desirable path.

Preparatory Rituals

How well you predict the outcome of future events depends on how much you practice doing it and how you prepare for it. Because you'll be tapping into powerful energy sources and receiving messages you'll need to interpret correctly, you must take a few safety measures before delving into divinatory practices.

Grounding Ritual

The first step is to perform a grounding meditation to prepare your mind, body, and soul for focusing on your intent and receiving the messages. There are many ways to do this, including the ever-popular root rituals often recommended for beginners. Here is a simple grounding root ritual you can perform:

1. Sit in a comfortable position with your feet planted firmly on the ground.
2. Slowing your breath, bring your awareness to your feet, and feel the ground beneath them.
3. Close your eyes and visualize natural energy taking the form of roots around your feet and traveling up your legs by growing roots.
4. Imagine the roots growing longer and stronger, holding you firmly in place.
5. Let this centered state relax you, and when it does, open your eyes.

Protection Ritual

The next step is to perform a protection spell to keep the negative influences away during your divinatory ritual. A great way for beginners to protect themselves is through a visualization technique which requires very few tools. In fact, you don't even have to use anything other than your imagination for the following method. If you want to use anything else, you can choose something as simple as a black candle, a picture of a black cat, or black and white crystals. Here is how to perform this protection ritual:

1. Start by relaxing your mind and body through deep breathing or a simple meditation technique.

2. Next, visualize a bright orb of light emerging at your feet and enveloping your entire body. Feel free to make the orb any color or shape you like, using your imagination.
3. Imagine the orb slowly filling your body with protective energy. Feel how it's reassuring you and letting you know that you will be safe spiritually during the divination ritual and that no negative energy will be able to harm you.
4. Finish the ritual with positive affirmations as a further reminder of your strength and power. The more confident you are in your ability to protect yourself, your shield will become stronger.

Cleansing Your Tools, Space, and Body

You should also think about cleansing your space, your tools, and yourself from any negative energy that may influence your results. When it comes to energetically cleansing your tools, the method you use depends on the type of tools you need to purify. Clear stones, crystal balls, water, mirrors, and other shining surfaces used for scrying are typically cleansed by being left out under the moonlight overnight. Other tools can be cleaned by passing them over the smoke of a black or white candle or the incense of your choice.

The latter method also applies to the divination space you'll use. Divinatory practices are commonly performed in an open space under the moon's protection during the night. So, if you opt for this method, nature will take care of shielding your sacred space. However, depending on how strictly you want to follow the ancient Egyptian traditions, your primary concern should be purifying your body. According to the ancient practice, a person set to perform divination had to undergo a 3-day cleansing process. This meant abstaining from unhealthy vices and behavior (including the use of alcohol), eating food that promoted purification, and taking cleansing baths.

Preparing Your Space

Preparing your space will help you set the appropriate mood for your divinatory ritual. The amount of natural light you have in your sacred space while performing divination will affect your mood and your ability to interpret the messages you'll receive. This light can come from candles (if you are performing the ritual indoors), the sun (which can be used both outdoors and indoors), or the moon (typically used for night scrying). Apart from the specific divination method you opt for, the amount of light will also depend on your preferences. It's okay if you don't know how much you'll need, as you'll figure it out as you practice.

The same goes for the ambient sound. Some practitioners prefer silence when looking for answers, while others use music to relax and reach a trance-like state. Certain essential oil and incense can also help you set the perfect mood for a relaxing session. Herbs were commonly used for similar purposes used by ancient Egyptians.

Regardless of how you prepare for a divination ritual, the space you choose for it must be away from all the distractions of the modern world. All electronic devices should be turned off (you can put your phone in flight mode), and any artificial lights should be turned off. You may also want to prepare a pen and a piece of paper in case you want to write down the answers so you can analyze them later. This will be particularly helpful if you are new to divination techniques or are performing dream divination.

Common Divinatory Methods in Ancient Egypt

The primary divinatory methods used in ancient Egypt were trance, water, and oil scrying, fire messages, divination via knots, and dream interpretation. Here are how these methods worked in ancient Egypt and how you can perform them today.

Dream Divination

The ancient Egyptians believed that dreams had the power to convey messages from the spiritual world, which is why they used dream interpretation as a common divination method. If you want the future to reveal itself through your dreams, you should address a specific guide from which you want to receive the answers. They'll visit you in your sleep and convey messages you'll interpret when you awake. Here is how to do this method:

1. Prepare for sleep with your preferred relaxation method by removing all distractions like light and sound sources.
2. Light a black candle and say a prayer to your guide, asking them for the answers you seek about your future.
3. Make sure you thank them for any messages they send and, if you wish, prepare a small offering.
4. Leave a piece of paper and a pen at your bedside and go to bed without using any electronic device.

5. You may wake right after receiving a message from the spiritual world, in which case, you write down what you saw right away.
6. Even if you don't wake up right away, you may still want to record the messages in the morning, even if you know what they mean. This can serve you as a reference for future divinatory practices.

Using Knots for Divination

The use of knots in witchcraft originated in Ancient Egypt, and there is evidence that knots were often employed for divination purposes. This typically involved making an amulet from the knots and using it for interpretation. With the following method, you can also perform a quick divinatory ritual:

1. Find 16 individual, foot-long threads - 4 white, 4 red, 4 blue, and 4 green ones.
2. Gather the threads into one band and stain the band with a drop of red coloring. Traditionally the practitioner's blood was used for staining, but any red color will do.
3. Bind the band around your wrists, get into a relaxed state and focus on the question you want to be answered.
4. The band will act as a vessel for the messages, so focus on your hand when expecting the answers.
5. Visualize the messages in the form of energy traveling from your arm toward your body and head.
6. Once they reach your mind, it will be up to you to interpret them.

Moon Divination

The ancient Egyptians acknowledged the moon's influence on human life in both a physical and a spiritual sense. They believed that the full moon enhanced the impact of whatever actions you took, and it reflected your intentions perfectly. Because of this, they were more than ready to use the reflection of the moon for divinatory purposes, and such is the case with the following method:

1. Start by finding a place where you'll perform the ritual outdoors at the full moon. If you can't go outside, stand by an open window where the moon shines in, and you can see its likeness.
2. Gather a bowl of water, incense, and a censer for holding the burning incense.

3. Take the items from above to the place you've chosen for divination.
4. Place the incense in the censer on the ground and stand straight, holding the bowl of water. Stand in a position where you can see the moon's reflection on the water's surface.
5. Recite the following invocation 7-9 times, either in your mind or aloud, depending on what helps you focus more:

   "For you, great Moon, the leader of the stars,

   you who helped form them,

   listen now to what I have to say.

   Follow the words of my mouth, and reveal your secrets to me!"
6. Now, carefully consider anything you may hear, see, or otherwise perceive. If you are lucky, the Moon goddess herself will appear and present you with the answers to your question.
7. You may also receive other signs, such as the movement in the water or the appearance of a key part of your answer on the moon's surface.

Oil Scrying

Another common form of divination in ancient Egypt involved the use of an oil lamp. Lamps used for divination were typically white, free from any red colors, and lit in dark, serious places. Later on, this was replaced by the use of oil scrying, which is essentially the combination of water scrying and the oil lamp method. Just as lamps were forbidden to touch the ground, it's recommended not to place any vessel with oil onto the ground. The steps for this method are similar to the moon scrying technique, except you'll be using vegetable oil. Unlike water, oil doesn't break the image, so you'll be able to focus for longer. Make sure you pour the oil into the bowl very slowly to prevent it from becoming cloudy, as this will hinder your ability to interpret spiritual messages.

Additional Tips for Divination

Whether it's part of ancient Egyptian or any other magic practice, divination is a skill that requires a lot of practice to master. That said, there are a few ways to advance your learning journey. Starting by setting a broad intention, no matter how tempting it is, it is recommended to seek a direct answer. It's more than likely that you will not receive one even after plenty of practice as a beginner, but you won't even notice whether you do or not. Remember, you will experience things you've never seen before, which makes interpreting any message challenging, not to mention that you can't be sure in which form the response will come. Setting a specific intention will not give you a specific answer - and can even block messages that may hold the answer you seek.

For example, you can set an intention like this:

"My mind and heart are now open to any messages that guide me toward my future goal."

An intention like this communicates that you want positive or constructive messages regarding your current life but are open to whatever form you may receive them. Once you practice scrying a little more, you get more familiar with the type of message you receive, and you learn how to interpret them. Then you can move on to asking for answers to more specific issues. However, you still can't ask direct questions, as the answers will not be direct either. An example of a more specific intention could be:

"My mind and heart are now open to receiving any messages regarding my current financial status."

Deep breathing can help you achieve and maintain the perfect focus - and if it doesn't, you can still do a few things to maintain concentration. With some methods, you can close your eyes to close out any visual distractions, whereas, with others (like with scrying), you'll need to keep your eyes unfocused, allowing your mind to focus instead. You can do this by softening your gaze.

Once the focus is transferred to your mind's eye, you may begin to see symbols, shapes, or even living beings appear. Keep in mind that it may take 5-10 minutes of gazing before anything appears, so make sure you wait at least that long. Don't second guess what you see - even if it seems that what you have seen, heard, or otherwise perceived was the product of your imagination. It's more likely that the gut feeling you got was right, no matter how random it may seem, and it turns out to be a message you'll benefit from later on.

Since you'll probably be in a deep meditative state while performing divination, your conscious mind may need a little help to remember what you've experienced. It's recommended to keep a journal in which you record your experience. When scrying, make sure you do this after the session, so you don't have to look away from the surface. Apart from writing it down, you can also record your session using your phone to ensure you don't miss out on any part of the message. If you are going to do this, practice describing every part of your experience aloud. This way, you'll know what you are listening to when you replay the recording.

Chapter 9: Sacred Plants and Herbs

Another form of magical practice which originated in ancient Egypt is plant magic. Egyptians used sacred plants and herbs for healing rites, love spells, self-empowerment rituals, and tools for warding off negative influences. They believed that each plant has its own magical effect, and knowing the strengths of a specific plant is key to successfully using them in spellwork. Because of this, herbs can enhance your practice, even if you don't have too much experience. Plant magic will always have the desired result. You just have to know how to employ it correctly.

The magic within the plants, and the speed with which they act, allow you to use them more efficiently than any other magical art form. When casting a spell, you find the plants or herbs that possess the properties you want to incorporate into your work, and your spell will be instantly empowered with natural magic. This chapter contains an extensive list of powerful plants and herbs used in ancient Egyptian spell work and their spiritual meaning and magical purposes.

Ancient Egyptian Herbs and Plants

Acacia

You'll recognize Acacia trees by their characteristic thorns, segmented leaves, and pea-like legumes. In ancient times, Egyptians associated Acacia with deities like Ra, Diana, Osiris, and Astarte - all known for being aligned with powerful elements such as the air or the sun itself. It's believed that Acacia carries distinctively masculine energy, which is why it's often used for protection spells and for drawing psychic energy for powerful spellwork.

As a beginner, you can use Acacia to enrich your practice by incorporating them into your ritual while you are still learning. One way to use this is to extract the gum from the tree by cutting the branch and simply letting it drip out, making it a base for your favorite incense. You can also combine the plant with sandalwood and make a relaxing incense you use during your preparatory meditation. If you want to reach out to a soul inhabiting the spiritual world or use your power more confidently, you should burn Acacia leaves on charcoal while focusing on your intention.

African Violet

For the ancient Egyptians, African Violet represented the feminine counterpart of Acacia's masculine energy. Its power is said to be aligned with the energy of Venus and the water element. This small plant is known for its round leaves and bright or deep purple flowers.

You may use it for spiritual protection during spellwork or simply to enhance your spirituality and those who live in your home. Remember that, unlike other violet varieties, African Violet isn't an edible plant. In fact, its flowers can be highly toxic for pets and small children, so make sure to keep them away from them and avoid ingesting them.

Catnip

Catnip was used to attract good luck in cat magic.
Robert Flogaus-Faust, CC BY 4.0 <https://creativecommons.org/licenses/by/4.0>, via Wikimedia Commons: https://commons.wikimedia.org/wiki/File:Nepeta_cataria_3_RF.jpg

Due to their fascination with cat magic, ancient Egyptians made many magical associations with these four-legged creatures. One of these was the use of catnip in cat magic, which was typically performed to attract good luck and benevolent spirits. It has small purple flowers and leaves similar to mint. You can use it to enhance happiness and promote beauty. You can hang it in a satchel above head level to induce beauty and happiness. Another great way to use catnip satchels is in conjunction with rose petals. Mix these two, scoop up some of the mixture into your hands, and let it warm up. After that, you should hold someone else's hand. This person will become one of your best friends. While catnip can be beneficial for cats in some quantities, it can be toxic in high doses.

Chamomile

Chamomile is one of the most ancient herbs used in healing magic. Due to its delicate yet bright white flower, ancient Egyptians associated this plant with the sun's deities. It was often used to invoke the god Ra for its healing powers when they needed remedies for communicable diseases like malaria. Ancient Egyptians also used chamomile for mummification because they believed it could help protect the deceased from malicious spirits brought on by insects. Dried plants were added to the bath for relaxation and cleansing before rituals and spell work.

In ancient times, practitioners would even plant chamomile alongside other, more sensitive plants they needed for their work. This ensures the other plant gets all the nutrients needed to thrive. Chamomile is believed to attract wealth and prosperity because fresh plants smell like green apples - and green is the color associated with wealth and material gains. Brew a strong chamomile tea and wash your hands in it before you perform any spell work related to money, work progress, etc. You can also drink a milder version of the tea or place loose dried flowers under your pillow for vision-inducing dream work.

Cinnamon

Also known as sweet wood, cinnamon was another plant used in ancient Egyptian healing and protective magic practices. They used cinnamon oil in beauty rituals, rites for healing scars, enhancing spirituality and psychic abilities, and as part of the concoction used for the mummification process. They also incorporated cinnamon oil and bark into protection and love spell work.

While nowadays, it's typically used for the tantalizing aroma it adds to foods, cinnamon can still find its way into modern spellwork. You can use both the bark and the oil to strengthen love bonds and familial relationships. The oil can also serve as an empowering anointment for candles used during rituals, spells, and meditative practice to enhance your spiritual and psychic powers.

Cypress

Cypress is an evergreen tree known for its longevity, which is why in ancient Egypt, it was considered a symbol of eternity, and it was even said to grant immortality. Its wood was used to make sarcophagi and in various rituals to prolong life. Cypress oil was incorporated into healing magic or spellwork to ward off evil spirits during rituals and ceremonies.

You can also find cypress oil and use this to protect yourself and your work. Its aroma has a comforting effect, which will help you relax and focus on manifesting your intent. Taking a small twig of cypress to the grave of your loved ones will let them know that they are still loved, which will help both of you to move on.

Daisy

Daisies are known for their dainty white flowers and yellow seedbeds. In ancient Egypt, the flowers represented femininity and were also associated with the sun and the water element. Daisies were often offered to female deities when asked for guidance. They were used for divinatory practices and love spells, giving way to modern acts, such as the "love me, love me, not" divination.

You can also use dried flowers to offer to the deity of your choice, scatter them around for love spells, or put them under the loved one's bed. Be careful when doing this, as some people are allergic to daisies. Don't ingest any part of the plant either, nor should you let small children or animals eat them. Several toxic substances lead to vomiting, nausea, and other digestion issues.

Dandelion

Like chamomile, dandelion was also associated with sun deities due to how much young flowers resemble this heavenly body. Its main flower consists of a large group of small needle-like individual flowers. These become translucent when they mature and are easily blown away by the wind and the seeds. Because of this, Egyptians associated dandelions with the air element and believed the tiny flowers to be able to carry messages across this world and the spiritual one.

Nowadays, people use mature flower heads to make a wish before blowing off the seeds, but this can also be used in magical practice. For example, you can do this if you are trying to get a deity to work with you. Or you can simply offer dried younger flowers to the sun gods. Tea made from dandelion roots can also be used in healing magic, whereas tea made from flowers will enhance your psychic abilities and enable spiritual communication.

Elder

The Elder was considered a very powerful source of magic in ancient Egypt. Its flowers have five petals (and the same number of sepals), forming a tiny green star when they come together. Since the number 5 was associated with many mystical happenings, Elderflower was used for a broad range of magical acts. This included spellwork and rituals to find a connection to the natural kingdom, crossing the gateway to the spiritual realm, and healing magic. They may also have used it to represent life's cycle and to celebrate new beginnings after a meaningful period had come to an end. Elder trees were sometimes planted near graves to keep away the evil spirit.

You can nowadays use Elder flowers and bark for protection, grounding, and meditative relaxation, and incorporate these into your practice in several ways. Elder is said to open the mind, so you become open to different kinds of spiritual messages and see things in a more positive light. This can also be helpful in magic meant to heal emotional traumas and open the heart while ensuring it's shielded from further trauma. If you have a larger garden, you can even grow an Elder tree, as it will protect you and your property from harm and bad luck. Berries and mature leaves can be harvested and hung up on doorways for spiritual protection or warding off evil intent sent your way.

Henbane

Recognizable for its large white flowers and green leaves sporting deep white veins, henbane is a plant with powerful properties. Ancient Egyptians used this plant's leaves, flowers, and seeds for healing magic meant to treat mortal injuries. They praised this plant for its pain-relieving effects, which we know results from a compound that relaxes the nervous system. Beginning from the times of the ancient Egyptians, henbane was also one of the ingredients of flying ointment, an incredibly powerful magical tool.

Nowadays, henbane is only recommended to use in healing rituals when you want to invoke spiritual protection for someone who is ill or injured. Don't ingest the plant, as it's extremely toxic and can lead to respiratory and heart issues, even in small amounts. With children and animals, ingesting this plant can have dire consequences.

Lavender

Lavender is known for its fragrant flowers, often used for refreshing the contents of wardrobes, as a relaxation tool, or as an ingredient in natural hygiene products. The ancient Egyptians had similar uses for lavender, as they incorporated it into various aromatherapy treatments and even the mummification process. Lavender was also recorded as a great pain reliever and anti-inflammatory agent to treat burns and wounds. Egyptians included lavender in their magic spells when trying to find a solution for insomnia, indigestion, and many other ailments and symptoms.

In modern times, you can also place dried lavender under your pillow to have a more relaxed sleep. You'll either process messages you receive during the day or find them through dream divination. The calming effect of lavender promotes self-acceptance and harmony. Lavender ashes are a great cleanser that you can use during your preparatory practices. Scattering these ashes around or creating them before your spellwork will ward off malicious influences and the evil spirits themselves. You can also hand a branch of flowers outside your home for added protection.

Lotus

In ancient Egypt, the lotus was believed to have beneficial powers for protection and love. At that time, this plant was viewed as a symbol of spiritual life; according to some sources, it may even have been considered a gateway to the center of the universe. Ancient Egyptians used this plant as an offering to the gods during religious and magic ceremonies. Lotus oil was a traditional wedding gift for the newlyweds as it was believed to help grow and protect their love.

Nowadays, lotus oil can be used in love magic spells, spiritual relaxation, and self-love. Its relaxing aroma can help you become more confident in your abilities, especially in psychic divination. It also promotes spiritual growth and cleansing, truth revelations, and the finding of good luck. You may also use it to calm your mind and during a dream divination session.

Mint

Mint is known for its green, aromatic leaves, which are often used for teas and to enhance the flavor of meals. However, ancient Egyptians often used mint in spells and rituals to encourage love, wealth, and prosperity. Also, mint was believed to help keep out evil spirits and empower practitioners spiritually. It was also used in healing magic to relieve muscle fatigue and digestion issues, just as it's still used today in modern aromatherapy practices.

A cup of mint tea in the morning can bring you good fortune throughout your day, so feel free to drink it anytime you feel down on your luck. Dry out the leaves, and place them over the bed of a person who is ill or injured, and it will ward off negative energy and allow the person to recoup. You can also place dry mint leaves under your pillow before going to sleep. It will provide protection during dream divination. Its relaxing aroma will also enhance your ability to interpret the messages you receive during your sleep.

Mugwort

Mugwort is a herb that promotes psychic development and the enrichment of divinatory practices, particularly during sleep. This plant was also used in ancient Egypt to protect against evil spirits and physical injuries. Due to its ability to neutralize poisons, mugwort was part of Egyptian healing magic practice. It's also recorded to have been used to relieve digestive issues.

In modern times, practitioners use mugwort mainly as a tea prepared to get in the mood for receiving psychic visions, divinatory messages, and prophetic dreams. Dried mugwort can also be smoked or incorporated into ointments and applied to the skin. Depending on the dosage, these applications can help varying degrees of psychoactive effects. Bear in mind that, for this reason, you have to be careful with the dosage and shouldn't let animals or children consume it.

Myrtle

Known for its sweet pink flowers, myrtle was considered one of the greatest tools for love magic in ancient Egypt. Practitioners who wanted to enact a love spell and strengthen their bond with their partner would wear a wreath made of fresh myrtle flowers during the spell. This tree was also associated with fertility and was employed in spells that either encouraged conception or ensured it wouldn't happen quickly (hence why many new brides wear it during their wedding day).

If you want to keep your love life exciting, you can also wear a myrtle wreath. You can give small flower branches to people you want to become friends with. To maintain a youthful appearance and agility, you should drink myrtle tea for 3 days in a row. Growing myrtle in your yard will help you attract wealth, fertile ideas, and new opportunities through which you can persevere.

Rosemary

Like lavender, rosemary is also an incredibly aromatic herb with multiple magical and non-magical properties. It's recognizable for its small spiky leaves that sit on strong branches. Apart from its ability to enhance flavors in the kitchen as a dried loose herb, rosemary is also used in oil infusion form to relieve aches. In ancient Egypt, rosemary was an inevitable part of love spells, was considered an aphrodisiac and protection rites, and was also favored for its cleansing abilities. You can burn rosemary leaves to purify your space and body before spellwork. Placed in a bath, rosemary has a spiritually invigorating effect and will help you chase away negative thoughts. Placing rosemary in a sachet near the entrance of your loved one's home will fortify your relationship, leaving no place for jealousy and mistrust. You can also place rosemary under their pillow to make them think of you more often. Or you can put it under your pillow for deeper relaxation during sleep, enhancing dream visions and warding off nightmare-inducing influences.

Sage

According to ancient Egyptian lore, sage can help ward off evil and was often used in cleansing and other magical ceremonies. Sage has grayish-green juicy leaves, which were dried and either used as a loose herb or burned as part of a smudging ritual. It was said to bring good luck and even help gather the wisdom needed for successful spellwork. Egyptian healing magic has also seen its benefits, as it was often used for its anti-inflammatory properties and to empower one's mind, body, and spirit to help overcome illnesses and injuries.

Apart from adding a great aroma to your dishes, you can also incorporate sage into your own contemporary Egyptian spellwork. You can use it for smudging or simply burn it as incense during preparatory or meditative practices. It will help you overcome grief and traumatic events and build up your emotional and spiritual strength. Use it in your cleansing ceremonies to add purity, especially to your spirit, and to rid yourself and your space of negative spirits and energies. Burning sage is generally recommended if you are new to magical practices and are looking for quick and easy ways to eliminate negative influences that can hinder your learning journey.

Vervain

Vervain is another plant with both cleansing and protective properties. In ancient Egypt, it was used to purify a sacred ritual space and to ensure that all those who cast the spell were protected from evil influences. There is also evidence that it was used in healing magic and was said to be particularly effective for digestive and kidney issues.

You can dry its purple flowers and sprinkle them around your home and ritual site to keep away evil spirits. You can also prepare tea from the loose vervain herbs to soothe your digestive system or use this brew for magical purposes. Drink it before your divination practice or astral work, and your ability to interpret spiritual messages will increase. You can also juice the fresh plant and incorporate it into love spells and potions. It will also enhance your psychic abilities, but be careful with the dosage, as too much of it can cause hallucinations.

Chapter 10: Ancient Egyptian Spells and Rituals

In this chapter, you will find a few Egyptian spells for various purposes like protection, love, abundance, and healing. Keep in mind that this is just one way you can perform these spells. They can be altered in any way you see fit. You'll find step-by-step instructions for different forms of spells, rituals, prayers, and baths.

Spell for Protecting Against Food Poisoning

In Ancient Egypt, food poisoning was believed to have been caused by enemies. If someone suspected that their food was poisoned, they would perform a ritual before eating. The spell was based on the principle of retribution and turned the curse on whoever cast the spell in the first place. To perform this spell, you need to say the following before eating:

"*O Sakhmet of yesterday, Widget of today,*

You came and replenished my table,

Just as you did for your father when you came forth from the cult city of Pe.

Protect us with that papyrus wand of life, which is in your hand,

In that name of yours of Wadjet.

Shoot your arrow against all the food of him who shall speak against me

By means of any evil matters.

Let a slaughter be made of them like the time when you overpowered the enemies of Re in the primordial age, in the name of your of Sakhmet.

Your offerings belong to me."

You can now eat your food without any fear of poisoning. This spell was also meant to give you a long life by protecting you from any harm that could have been intended by your enemies.

Love Spell

When it comes to love spells, the caster needs to burn different types of offerings in the bathhouse and write the following on the walls:

"I adjure you, earth and waters, by the demon who dwells on you and (I adjure) the fortune of this bath so that, as you blaze and burn and flame, so burn her (the woman targeted) whom (the mother of the woman targeted) bore until she comes to me..."

You also need to include the names of the gods and magical words you will recite when you perform your spell. The spell also includes the following words:

"Holy names, inflame in this way and burn the heart of her..."

If you cast this spell to get someone to fall in love with you, you continue to say this until they do. If you are casting a spell on behalf of someone else, the person who is the focus of the ritual will eventually fall in love with them.

Another love spell to win her involves rubbing a tick from a dead dog onto your loins. This is a simple spell but is believed to be effective. Once a tick bites something, it does not fall away easily unless it is pulled or killed by an insecticide. This would symbolize your new relationship with the person you love.

Protection Spells

Negative energy, angry gods, spiteful demons, spirits, and other magic users can cause bad luck, misfortune, sickness, and many other ailments and accidents. Magic offered a defense mechanism against these ills. Several spells were performed using magical implements, special foodstuffs, talismans, and figurines. Hippo tusks were used to carve magic knives that were specifically intended to protect the children against spells and other dangers that could cause them harm, like snakes. Hippo talismans were very popular since they possessed potent power that could protect the young ones in particular.

Ivory wands were also used to provide a protective circle around the place where a woman would give birth or nurse her child. The wands were inscribed with the dangerous beings that the magician invoked to protect the mother and child. They were portrayed as strangling, stabbing, or biting evil forces that foreigners or snakes represented.

Shouting, stamping, and making a loud noise with drums, rattles, and tambourines were also believed to drive away hostile forces that could cause harm to vulnerable women. Pregnant women and children were also at risk of being attacked by dark forces and needed protection. That's where this spell came in handy.

Amulets have long been used for protection and are shaped like or engraved with depictions of animals and gods. They can also be inscribed with symbols and words to add power and enhance a spell - different animals/gods/royals will provide different types of protection and enhancements. However, if your spell was bent on causing harm to someone, the god rejected it. Therefore, you had to define your intention to avoid tempting the gods. All intentions were supposed to be valid for effective results.

Magical Healing

Different types of diseases were believed to have been caused by spirits, so healing was treated as magical science. Administration of medicines and nursing care were usually accompanied by specific rituals meant to eliminate the pathogenic agents responsible for causing the illness. When children suffered illnesses believed to be caused by evil spirits, the powers of the great god would be invoked by the high priest, and the patient would suddenly become well. Magicians, priests, and physicians all believed in magical powers.

You can attract demons to yourself when bad energy or negative things surround you. Spells can be used to get rid of negativity or evil spirits once they have arrived. Dung was long used in Ancient Egypt to draw out the demon from the body, but honey is also good for warding off evil (and it is not as messy as dung). Images of the evil spirit can be drawn and then destroyed to ward off evil or consume its power so that it becomes powerless. Inscribing healing and protective spells on amulets and statues was another spell performed by the healers.

Several spells included speeches that were recited by a doctor or the patient. Healing was to follow strict guidelines, and the body was supposed to be examined in a certain way. The results were to be interpreted first before treatments were performed. In each organ of the body, there are vessels, and magicians or priests would lay their fingers on the patient to feel the pulse of the heart.

Remedy for Headache

When someone suffered from a terrible headache, a certain spell was performed to address the situation. To perform this, one was supposed to obtain seven threads from a garment, which were made into seven knots. These knots were placed on the left foot of the sick person. The spell caster would recite the following words.

"My head, my head," said Horus.

"The half of my head (= migraine), the half of my head," said Thoth.

"Act for me, mother Isis and Aunt Nephthys!

Give me your head in exchange for my head, the half of my head!"

(Isis speaks): *"Just as I have seen these people (= human sufferers), so = I have heard these gods (Horus and Thoth) saying to me on behalf of my son Horus.*

'Let there be brought to me your head in exchange for my head.'

You should indicate your gratitude about how the threads brought from the edge of the garment will cure the headache. When word of the issues reaches the gods, a cure will be found.

Magic for Snake Bite

A snake bite often puts the patient's life in danger, and Sekhmet would threaten to cause consequences to the fabric of the world for the curse of the snake bite. He would recite the following prayer to ask for healing.

"*The sun barque is at rest and does not proceed,*

The sun is still in the same spot as yesterday.

The nourishment is without a ship; the temple is barred,

There the disease will turn back the disturbance

To yesterday's location."

This prayer was meant to protect the patient by blocking any potential harm that could lead to loss of life. The spirits would block the effects of the dark spirits to protect a life.

Daily Worship

Daily worship of the god and goddesses was another crucial ritual performed in places of worship. Each temple was dedicated to a god or goddess, and the Egyptians believed temples were sacred since the gods or goddesses lived there. Because of this, only priests were allowed to enter the temples to make rituals consisting of food offerings, drinks, and clothing to honor and appease the gods. Farmers would bring portions of their harvest to the temple to honor the deities. Every aspect of life in ancient Egypt was based on the beliefs and power of the gods.

Daily Offering Ritual

A daily offering ritual was meant to please the gods and goddesses and ask for protection. This ritual is still relevant today, and it consists of different steps you should follow if you want to perform it. The first step you should take is to burn incense before visiting your shrine. Open the shrine that is usually sealed by a cord. Remove the cord that is tied around the door knobs.

The individual performing the ritual must bow in front of the picture of the deity. They should kiss the ground, and this gesture is followed by raising arms while singing the ideal hymn for the ritual. This is followed by the offerings of scented oil and incense. When you visit the inner shrine, you must repeat the previous stages.

The main offering of the goddess is performed inside the shrine. Wrap the image of the god using four lengths of cloth; each must have a different name. You must provide your image with scented oil, black (lead), and green (copper) eyepaint. When you finish performing the ritual, you should leave the shrine. Make sure you sweep away your footprints and offer incense, natron, and water.

This is a daily offering ritual; you can perform it even if there are no issues you want to solve. It is meant to appease the gods and goddesses, so they continue protecting you against evil spells. When the gods are happy, you will get blessings, making your life much more enjoyable.

Preparations for Spells and Rituals

For magic spells to succeed, specific preparations were necessary, and it was a good idea to avoid unlucky days. Depending on the ritual you want to perform, you must choose the appropriate day, time, and place to do it. In ancient Egypt, most rituals were performed at dawn or dusk, and they were done in dark places and specifically designed for such spiritual endeavors. The magician, ingredients, and medium chosen for failure to uphold a high purity level meant that your ritual could not succeed. If the moon was used as the medium, then it was supposed to be pure. Ingredients and other implements used in the ritual had to be properly cleaned. Before going to the dark chamber for your spell, you had to sprinkle it with clean sand obtained from the great river. A clean vessel of pottery or bronze cup was used to hold pure water that would be used for the ritual.

Magic was an integral component of life in ancient Egypt, and it was used for protection, healing, birth, love, and even death. The gods performed their duties through heka (magic). The power of the gods was used to maintain balance and harmony in the universe. Different forms of magic were performed using various ingredients.

To the ordinary person, magic could be dangerous, and coming into contact with the tools used could be deadly. For instance, accidentally touching the scepter used by the magicians had to be resolved by invoking the king's spell.

Ancient Egyptian Deities A-Z

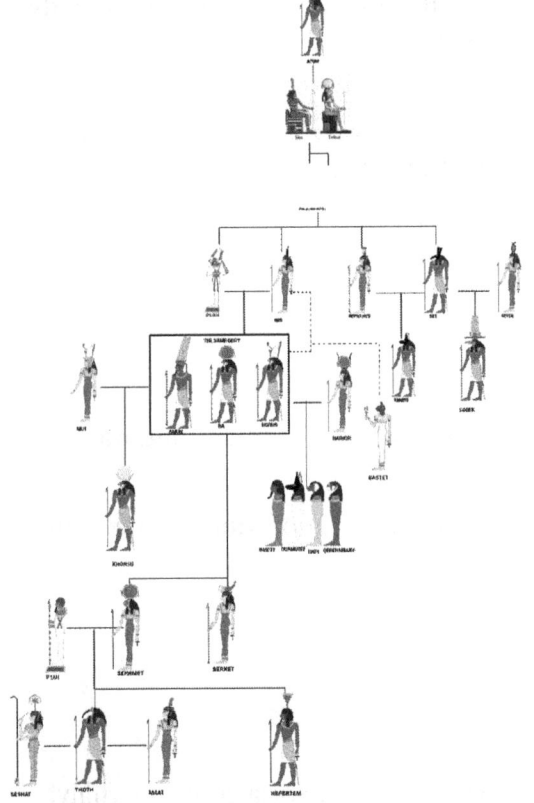

Egyptian gods family tree.
Lanewalker2, CC BY-SA 3.0 <https://creativecommons.org/licenses/by-sa/3.0>, via Wikimedia Commons: https://commons.wikimedia.org/wiki/File:ApproxEgyptianGodsFamilyTree.svg

A
A'ah
A god of the moon. Once called Iah and later called Knonsu.
Aken
Protected the souls of those who traveled by boat to the afterlife.
Aker
Custodian of the horizon from east to west.
Am-Heh
A god from the underworld who lived in a fiery lake.
Amenet
She supplied the dead with food and drink.
Ammit
Her hindquarters were that of a hippo, she had the body of a leopard, and her head was a crocodile.
Amun
The god of the sun and the air. He is the most popular and famous god in the ancient Egyptian Pantheon.
Amenhotep
The god of wisdom and healing.
Amunet
The wife of Amun.
Anat
The Female deity of love, sexuality, fertility, and war.
Anta
The Mother Goddess, often a part of Mut in some form.
Andjety
A god of fertility.
Anhur
The god of war.
Anqet
A part of the Nile river and also associated with fertility.
Anti
The hawk god of upper Egypt.

Anubis
Deity of the deceased.
Anuke
One of the oldest deities of the pantheon. She is the goddess of war.
Apedemak
Another war god who took the form of a lion.
Apep
The serpent demon of chaos.
Apis
The bull-shaped god of fertility.
Arensnuphis
Nubian god and Isis' companion.
Asclepius
The Greek god of healing – who was also worshiped by ancient Egyptians.
Ash
God of the Oases.
Astarte
Goddess of sexuality and fertility.
Aten
The sun deity and the personification of the sun disk.
Atum
The supreme lord of all gods. He is also the god of the sun.
Auf
One of the aspects of Atum.
B
Ba'al
The god of the storm.
Baalat Gebal
A protector goddess.
Babi
The god of virility and representative of male sexuality.

Banebdjedet
Another god of fertility – the ram god.
Ba-Pef
Bringer of spiritual terror.
Bastet
The cat goddess of fertility, protection, fertility, childbirth, and the secrets of women.
Bat
Bringer of fertility and success (also a cat deity).
Bennu
A bird deity associated with Ra, Osiris, and Atum.
Bes
Dwarf god of war, sexuality, childbirth, humor, and fertility.
Beset
Female counterpart of Bes.
Buchis
Depiction of Ka (a bull god).
C
Cavern Deities
They dwelled in the caves under the ground.
Celestial Ferryman
From the underworld, they transported souls across the river boundary.
D
Dedun
Overseer of other gods, offering them protection and resources.
Denwen
Fire deity – often represented by a dragon.
Duamutef
Responsible for the stomach of Horus that was stored in a jar.
E
Ennead
The nine gods of Heliopolis.

F
Fetket
The butler of Ra and also the god of bartenders.
Field of Reeds
Paradise in the afterlife.
Forty-Two Judges
The judges who met with the souls before the heart-weighing ceremony.
Four Sons of Horus
Qebehsenuef, Hapy, Imset, and Duamutef.

G
Geb
God of Earth and the sun of Tefnut and Shu.
Gengen Wer
Around since the beginning of the world – the divine goose.

H
Ha
Protector god of the Western Deserts.
Hapi
The god of fertility and the Nile silt.
Hapy
A protector god and a son of Horus.
Hardedef
King Khufu's son.
Hathor
Among the most significant and popular ancient Egyptian deities. Goddess of war, love, fertility, and the sky.
Hathor-Nebet-Hetepet
The Mother Goddess (Hathor) and the hand of Atum.
Hatmehit
A fish deity associated with rivers and deltas.
Haurun
Is a protector – but also brings death and destruction.

Hedetet

Deity of scorpions and can protect from their sting.

Heh and Hauhet

The frog and serpent deities that represent eternity and infinity.

Heqet

Deity of fertility and birth.

Heret-Kau

Protective goddess who was more powerful than all spirits.

Heka

Primordial form of power and deified form of magic and medicine.

Heryshaf

Ram god of fertility.

Heset

Goddess of food and beverages. She was typically associated with pleasure and beer.

Hetepes-Sekhus

An underworld cobra goddess who was a personification of Ra's eye.

Horus

Avian god that was associated with power, the sky, and the sun.

Hu

The god of the spoken word and the personification of Ra's first word.

I

Iah

A moon god who played an important role in the Egyptian calendar.

Iabet

Deity of fertility and birth.

Ihy

Deity of joy and music.

Imhotep

King Djoser's vizier and the architect of the step pyramid.

Imsety

A protector god and a son of Horus.

Ipy
A Mother Goddess who is associated with Osiris.
Ishtar
Deity of love, sexuality, and war.
Isis
A powerful Egyptian goddess of magic and healing.
Isis-Eutheria
The Greek version of Isis. Her tears formed the Nile river.
Iusaaset
A Mother Goddess and grandmother figure to the other deities.
Iw
A creation deity.
J
Jupiter-Amun
Roman version of Zeus-Amun.
K
Kabechet
Serpent goddess and the daughter of Anubis.
Kagemni
The vizier of King Sneferu – became the god of wisdom after his death.
Kek and Kauket
Gods of night and obscurity.
Khentekhtai
Crocodile god of Lower Egypt's Athribis.
Khentiamentiu
Abydos' god of fertility.
Khenmu
Early Upper Egyptian patron god of potters.
Khepri
An aspect of Ra, who was symbolized by the scarab beetle.
Kherty
Ram-headed god of the Duat, the ancient Egyptian realm of the dead.

Khonsu

A god of the moon who was able to instantly heal the ill.

L

Lady of the Acacia

Grandmother of the deities; another name for Iusaaset. This title was later granted to Hathor.

Lady of the Sycamore

Another name for Hathor.

M

Maahes

Powerful god of the un who protected the innocent.

Maat

The goddess of justice, harmony, and truth. She was among the most significant deities in ancient Egypt.

Mafdet

An early goddess of justice. She declared judgment and was responsible for execution.

Mandulis

Nubian god of the sun – also worshipped in Ancient Egypt.

Mau

The cat of the gods and connected closely to Ra – the cat protected the Tree of Life when it was in danger.

Mehen

Serpent deity and protector of Ra.

Mehet-Weret

The cow deity, and one of the oldest goddesses.

Mehit

An early moon goddess, and is Anhur's consort.

Mekhit

A lioness goddess of war of Nubian origins.

Menhit

The representation of Ra's brow and the lioness and sun goddess.

Meretseger
Cobra deity of protection.

Merit
Musical goddess who could create order.

Meskhenet
Among the oldest ancient Egyptian deities. She was the goddess of childbirth and was thought to attend childbirths. She was responsible for creating the ka and breathing it into the body.

Mestjet
A goddess with the head of a lioness. She was one with the numerous aspects of the Eye of Ra.

Min
The Predynastic Period's god of fertility and the deity of the eastern deserts.

Mnevis
Mnevis was believed to be an aspect of Ra and the divine bull of Heliopolis.

Montu
The falcon god – associated with Horus and Ra.

Mut
This mother goddess played a minor role in early history. However, her significance grew when she later became Amun's wife.

N

Nebethetpet
This goddess was a deification of Atum's hand and was worshiped at Heliopolis.

Nefertum
He was initially one of Atum's aspects but later became known as the god of nice smells and perfume. Nefertum was particularly linked to aromatic flowers.

Nehebkau
This protective god was believed to unite the ka with the ba after an individual died. He was also responsible for uniting the ka with the body at birth.

Nehmetawy
This goddess was worshiped at Hermopolis and was thought to embrace the less fortunate.

Neith
Neith was one of the most popular and lasting ancient Egyptian deities. She was a creator goddess and was linked to Nun. Egyptians believed that she invented birth and was responsible for growth.

Nekhbet
This vulture goddess was linked to Wadjet – often called "The Two Ladies."

Nekheny
Falcon deity that protected.

Neper
The embodiment of corn and the god of grains.

Nephthys
She was among the first five children of Geb and Nut. A goddess of fertility and twin sister of Isis.

Nu and Naunet
The goddess of primordial chaos.

Nut
Wife of Geb and goddess of the primordial sky.

O

Ogdoad
The eight gods of creation: infinity (Heh and Hauhet), water (Nun and Naunet), hiddenness (Amun and Amaunet), and darkness (Kek and Kauket),

Onuris
A god of hunting and war.

Osiris
He was among the first five children of Geb and Nut. Osiris was also the judge of the dead.

P
Pakhet
The lioness goddess of hunting with the vengeful attributes of the goddess Sekmet and the justice and rightfulness of Isis.

Panebtawy
He was the deification of the king. He was Horus' son and represented Horus as a child. He was thought to be the child god.

Peteese and Pihor
Even though they were humans, these brothers were deified due to their link with Osiris. This link was built when they drowned in the Nile River. Ever since then, they have become local protective deities.

Ptah
Ptah was among the oldest ancient Egyptian gods and was believed to be the deity of Memphis, the governor of truth, and the creator of the universe.

Q
Qebehsenuef
Qebehsenuef was one of Horus' sons and was believed to be a protective god in the form of a hawk.

Qudshu
Even though she was a Syrian deity of love, she was worshipped by ancient Egyptian as the goddess of divine ecstasy and sexual pleasure.

R
Ra
The powerful god of the sun of the city of Heliopolis. The pyramids of Giza are linked to this god.

Raettawy
Raettawy was the female aspect of the sun god Ra.

Ra-Harakhte
A god in the form of a falcon that was a blend between Horus and Ra.

Renpet
Renpet was a goddess who deified the year, representing the passage of time.

S

Sah

Sah was an astral god who deified the constellation, Orion. When depicted alongside Sothis, the pair represented Osiris and Isis in their astral forms.

Sekhmet

Sekhmet was among the most important ancient Egyptian deities. She was portrayed as a lion-headed woman and was believed to be the deity of healing and destruction.

Serket

This protective goddess mainly protected against venom. She was also a funerary deity.

Set

The god of chaos, war, and storms.

T

Ta-Bitjet

She was the goddess responsible for safeguarding against venomous and deadly stings. She cast healing spells too.

Tasenetnofret

This protective goddess was a version of Hathor. She was also Horus's companion.

Tatenen

This protective Earth god was related to Ptah.

Taweret

She was the hippopotamus protective goddess of childbirth and fertility. She was also believed to be Bes' consort.

Tayet

She was the weaving Goddess, and she was responsible for supplying clothes and textiles, and mummifications.

Tefnut

The Goddess of moisture and Atum Ra's daughter. She was often portrayed as a lioness or a serpent with the head of a lion.

Tenenit

She was the goddess of beer, brewing, and giving birth.

Thoth
Deity of words, wisdom, and integrity. Some Egyptologists suggest that he was initially a lunar god.

Tjenenyet
This protective goddess was worshiped in Hermonthis. She was also Montu's (the god of war) consort.

Tree Goddesses
The deities associated with trees, such as Hathor, Isis, and Nut.

Triads
A triad is a grouping of 3 significant deities.

Tutu
The god Tutu is known for keeping away from his adversaries and fighting against black magic and demons. He was part human, part snake, part lion, and had wings.

U

Uat-Ur
Deity of the Mediterranean Sea.

Unut
This goddess, with the head of a rabbit and the body of a serpent, was also known as "the rabbit goddess." She was believed to have been an aspect of Ra or Osiris.

W

Wadjet
Daughter of Ra and is a great protective goddess. She appeared in numerous stories about the Eye of Ra, and Weret-Hekau, which means "great magic," was among one of her many names.

Wadj-Wer
Also known as "The Great Green," Wadj-Wer was the deified form of delta lagoons, lakes, and swamps found near the Mediterranean Sea.

Waset
"The Powerful Female One" was one of Wast's titles. She was known as the city of Thebes' protective goddess.

Weneg

This protective god was closely related to the concept and goddess of Maat. He was believed to keep the peace between the heavens and Earth. He also carried the sky.

Wenenu

He was a hare god and the companion of Wenet, the snake goddess. He was thought to be an aspect of Ra or Osiris.

Wepset

Translates to "She Who Burns." She was known for destroying Osiris' adversaries.

Wepwawet

The name of this god means "Opener of the Ways," alluding to the belief that he cleared the path in wars. He also led the path to life after death, as well as during birth.

Werethekau

The name of this god translates to "Great of Magic." It is a title applied to numerous deities, including Isis and Wadjet.

Y

Yam

Although he was a Phonecian god, Yam made it to the ancient Egyptian pantheon through trade. He also appeared in Egyptian lore because of his battle with Set.

Z

Zenenet

One of the titles given to Isis, Zenenet was particularly used in Hermonthis.

Conclusion

As you have learned from this book, ancient Egyptian magic is one of the oldest known forms of magic. Magic was an essential part of the life of a person from Egypt. It was a fundamental part of medicine and was used by everyone from commoners to officials, royalty, pharaohs, as well as priests, and deities.

Protection magic was used in all elements of a person's life, from warding off evil spirits to curing injuries. The ancient Egyptians even went as far as to use it in rituals meant to ward off invading armies.

Just like in other cultures, in ancient Egypt, magic was either black or white. White magic was good magic that would protect, and black magic was magic that would damage or destroy. White magic could protect babies during birth and mothers during pregnancy; it could promote love or protect those journeying in other worlds.

Heka was the god of magic in ancient Egypt. He was, essentially, the personification of magic, and his name is actually the Egyptian word for magic. Magic was such a fundamental part of ancient Egyptian medicine that physicians were called the "priests of Heka."

Magic permeated every part of ancient Egyptian religious life. One of the primary ancient Egyptian deities, Isis, was one of the strongest magicians in Egypt, and her magical power was said to have been greater than that of the other gods. In fact, it was her magical power that was supposed to protect the kingdom of Egypt from enemies, and she had dominion over fate itself.

Tools used as part of ancient Egyptian magical practice include magic wands, ushabti figures, the sekhem scepter, and the Book of the Dead. However, perhaps the most prominent magical tools used by ancient Egyptians were magical amulets.

Many Egyptian symbols were believed to carry inherent magical power, and these symbols were made into amulets that were carried by individuals and placed with the dead in their tombs. Some well-known symbols and amulets include the ankh, the scarab, and the Wedjat eye. Other types of ancient Egyptian magic include divination and plant magic.

Over the years, ancient Egyptian magic and religion have been used in a variety of esoteric beliefs and societies, such as by the Hermetic Order of the Golden Dawn. However, despite these variations, it is still possible to find the history of true ancient Egyptian magic and religion – and this book has helped you to do exactly that.

Here's another book by Mari Silva that you might like

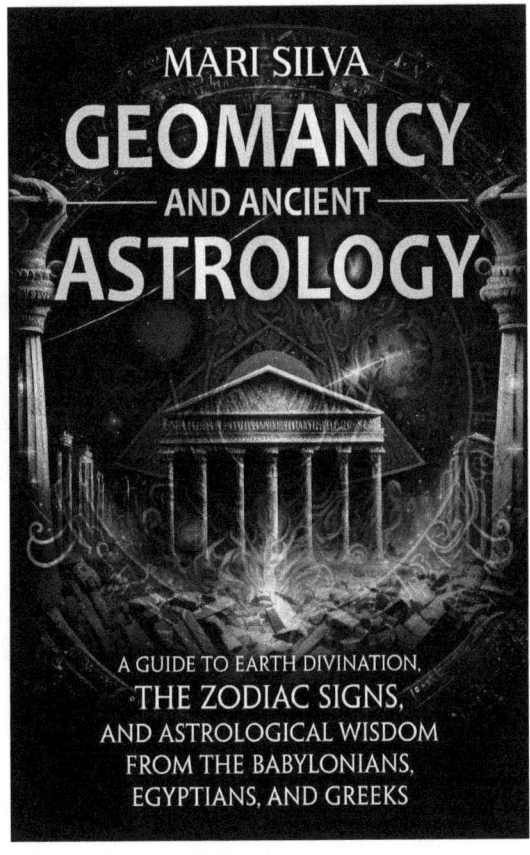

Your Free Gift
(only available for a limited time)

Thanks for getting this book! If you want to learn more about various spirituality topics, then join Mari Silva's community and get a free guided meditation MP3 for awakening your third eye. This guided meditation mp3 is designed to open and strengthen ones third eye so you can experience a higher state of consciousness. Simply visit the link below the image to get started.

https://spiritualityspot.com/meditation

References

42 laws of Maat under Kemet law. (n.d.). Blackhistoryheroes.com. http://www.blackhistoryheroes.com/2013/02/42-laws-of-maat-under-kemet-law-and.html

Ask-Aladdin. (n.d.). Ma'at Egyptian god - Ma'at the god of justice - AskAladdin. Egypt Travel Experts. https://ask-aladdin.com/egypt-gods/maat/

Atum [UC4GrfTi1FYF87_wJnPxaSyA]. (2021, May 9). 42 Laws Of Maat | Ancient Egyptian Bible | Origins of morality. Youtube. https://www.youtube.com/watch?v=DgPc90iqa8Y

December. (n.d.). 42 laws of Maat. The Xovia Collection. https://xoviacollection.com/blogs/heal-thy-self/48-laws-of-maat

Gill, N. S. (2010, May 18). Who Was Ma'at in Ancient Egypt? ThoughtCo. https://www.thoughtco.com/who-is-maat-119785

Ma'at. (n.d.). Egyptianmuseum.org. https://egyptianmuseum.org/deities-Maat

Maat. (n.d.). Ancientegyptonline.co.uk. https://ancientegyptonline.co.uk/maat/

maat | Egyptian religious concept. (n.d.). In Encyclopedia Britannica.

The 42 ideals of ma'at -. (2019, March 24). Kemet Experience. https://www.kemetexperience.com/the-42-ideals-of-maat/

The Editors of Encyclopedia Britannica. (2021). Maat. In Encyclopedia Britannica.

Wigington, P. (2009, August 6). Ma'at Egyptian goddess of truth and balance. Learn Religions. https://www.learnreligions.com/the-egyptian-goddess-maat-2561790

Ellison, T. (2021, June 15). Magic in the ancient world: Egyptian deities and uses. TheCollector. https://www.thecollector.com/magic-ancient-world-egyptian-deities/

Harris, E. (2016). Ancient Egyptian magic. Red Wheel/Weiser.

Mark, J. J. (2017). Magic in ancient Egypt. World History Encyclopedia. https://www.worldhistory.org/article/1019/magic-in-ancient-egypt/

Egyptian civilization - Myths - Creation myth. (n.d.). Historymuseum.Ca.

McLean, J. (n.d.). Ancient Egyptian religion. Lumenlearning.com https://courses.lumenlearning.com/suny-hccc-worldcivilization/chapter/ancient-egyptian-religion/

San-Aset. (2020, July 13). The seven principles of ma'at. Iseum Sanctuary. https://iseumsanctuary.com/2020/07/12/the-seven-principles-of-maat/

Themes, W. (2019, June 11). The Egyptian ceremony of the weighing of the heart. St James Ancient Art. https://www.ancient-art.co.uk/the-egyptian-cerimony-of-the-the-weighing-of-the-heart/

Alvar, J. (2020, March 22). *Worship of this Egyptian goddess spread from Egypt to England*. National Geographic. https://www.nationalgeographic.co.uk/history-and-civilisation/2020/03/worship-of-this-egyptian-goddess-spread-from-egypt-to-england

Apep (apophis). (n.d.). Ancientegyptonline.co.uk. https://ancientegyptonline.co.uk/apep/

Bastet (bast). (n.d.-a). Egyptianmuseum.org https://egyptianmuseum.org/deities-Bastet

Bastet (bast). (n.d.-b). Egyptianmuseum.org https://egyptianmuseum.org/deities-Bastet

Bastet (bast). (n.d.-c). Egyptianmuseum.org. https://egyptianmuseum.org/deities-Bastet

Caro, T. (2021, January 7). How to Know if a Goddess is Calling you? [Signs Explained]. *Magickal Spot*. https://magickalspot.com/is-goddess-calling-me/

Category:Maat-goddess (hieroglyph). (n.d.). Wikimedia.org. https://commons.wikimedia.org/wiki/Category:Maat-goddess_(hieroglyph)

Connecting with Neith? (n.d.). Reddit. https://www.reddit.com/r/witchcraft/comments/p2sjed/connecting_with_neith/

Cult of Isis. (n.d.). Wabash.edu http://persweb.wabash.edu/facstaff/royaltyr/AncientCities/web/rel%20372%20project/ISIS.htm

Deprez, G. (2021, April 24). *Goddess Isis: Fascinating facts about the mother of all gods*. TheCollector. https://www.thecollector.com/ancient-egyptian-goddess-isis/

Egyptian civilization - Myths - The divine family. (n.d.). Historymuseum.Ca.

Explore deities in ancient Egypt. (n.d.). Egyptianmuseum.org. https://egyptianmuseum.org/deities-overview

Fields, K. (2020, February 18). *Bastet: 9 ways to work with the Egyptian cat goddess of the home*. Otherworldly Oracle; FIELDS CREATIVE CONSULTING. https://otherworldlyoracle.com/bastet-egyptian-cat-goddess/

Fields, K. (2022, June 26). *Isis Goddess of Magic: 12 ways to work with her POWERFUL energy*. Otherworldly Oracle; FIELDS CREATIVE CONSULTING. https://otherworldlyoracle.com/isis-goddess/

Fulton, N. (2020). *Serqet: A bug, a brother, and a great big bomb*. Independently Published.

Geller. (2016, October 17). *Neith*. Mythology.net. https://mythology.net/egyptian/egyptian-gods/neith/

Gerges, F. A. (2021). *ISIS: A History*. Princeton University Press.

Hill, B. (2019, June 9). *Maat: Ancient Egyptian goddess of truth, justice and morality*. Ancient Origins. https://www.ancient-origins.net/history-ancient-traditions/maat-ancient-egyptian-goddess-truth-justice-and-morality-003131

Isis: Goddess symbols, correspondences, myth & offerings. (2021, July 2). Spells8. https://spells8.com/lessons/isis-goddess-worship/

Jay, N. (2020, December 1). *Neith – creator of the universe*. Symbol Sage. https://symbolsage.com/neith-egyptian-goddess/

Lesso, R. (2022, May 31). *Why was sekhmet important to ancient Egyptians?* TheCollector. https://www.thecollector.com/why-was-sekhmet-important-to-ancient-egyptians/

LibGuides: Bastet: About. (2021a). https://westportlibrary.libguides.com/bastet

LibGuides: Bastet: About. (2021b). https://westportlibrary.libguides.com/bastet

Maat. (n.d.). The Fitzwilliam Museum. https://fitzmuseum.cam.ac.uk/objects-and-artworks/highlights/context/tradition-and-change/maat

Ma'at. (n.d.). Enlightenment Through Hellfire https://scarletarosa.tumblr.com/post/631441701809029120/maat-egyptian-goddess-of-truth-justice-harmony

Maat – Egyptian Goddess of Justice. (2013, April 3). Crystal Vaults. https://www.crystalvaults.com/goddess-maat/

Maat symbol. (2018, July 2). Ancient Symbols. https://www.ancient-symbols.com/symbols-directory/maat.html

www.ingramcontent.com/pod-product-compliance
Lightning Source LLC
Chambersburg PA
CBHW051853160426
43209CB00006B/1284